# Just Because
# I Used To Could...

## Life Stories and Beyond

Lisa Batten Kunkleman

**Just Because
I Used To Could...**

Life Stories and
Beyond

This is a work of non-fiction, with the exception of the author's decision to change a name, time, or location due to memory lapse or to protect an identity.

Just Because I Used To Could...
Life Stories and Beyond
Copyright © 2019 Lisa Batten Kunkleman

All rights reserved. No part of this book may be used or reproduced in any manner whatsoever, except in the case of quotations included in reviews, without prior permission from the author.

For more information about Life Stories and Beyond
Go to: https://lifestoriesandbeyond.com
Facebook: Lisa Batten Kunkleman
Instagram: @lisakunk
Email lisakunk@msn.com to request author appearances or for other personal correspondence.

Layout and Editing by Rachelle McClintock, Ben Todys, Danielle Todys, Emma Hand, Kathy Brown, Mary Good, and Dan Kunkleman

Illustrations by Lois Ellis Batten
Cover Design by Ben and Danielle Todys
Life Stories Publishing Illustration by Jessica Jacks-Turkas

Manufactured in the United States
Life Stories Publishing, LLC
Charlotte, NC 28270

ISBN: 978-1-7331525-0-1
ISBN (eBook): 978-1-7331525-1-8

## Dedication

This book is dedicated in honor of my mother, Lois Ellis Batten, and in memory of my father, Wesley Carl Batten. They taught me how to love unconditionally and encouraged me to follow my own path. I'm eternally grateful for that freedom to explore all that the world has to offer. I thank you and love you both.

## Table of Contents

**Why Did I Write This Book?** ........................................... 1

**Healthy Living** ............................................................... 4
No Dairy, No Gluten, No Meat, Oh My! ........................... 5
Where are My Leg Warmers? ............................................ 8
Something's Wrong with Chewing a Smoothie ............. 11
Sometimes Ugly is Good for You .................................... 12

**Body Wisdom** ................................................................ 14
Mammogram: Making the Most of It .............................. 15
I'd Like to Change "The Change" .................................... 18
Blame My Muffin Top ....................................................... 21
Cicadas in My Head .......................................................... 24
Patent Pending .................................................................. 26
Another Thing My Knees Don't Like .............................. 29

**Nature is Never Boring** ................................................ 31
Bullying or Flirting? .......................................................... 32
You Swim with What? ...................................................... 35
Where Did All the Gators Go? ......................................... 37
Stray-Dar ............................................................................ 39
Rake the Lake .................................................................... 44
Winged Invasion ............................................................... 48

A Broom is My Snow Blower ................................................... 51

Eclipse Watching ..................................................................... 55

A Bathtub Full of Hurricane Prep Water ............................. 58

**Stuff and Beyond ................................................................ 61**

What's in Your Drawers? ....................................................... 62

One Man's Trash ..................................................................... 64

Consignment Worthy? ........................................................... 67

Mysterious Recycling Phenomenon .................................... 71

**Life, The Great Classroom ................................................ 73**

Rest in Peace ............................................................................ 74

Walnuts and My Tom Sawyer Moment .............................. 77

Squabble, Tiff, or Spat: Just Fix It ......................................... 80

And Evil is Her Name ............................................................. 83

Auditing Life ............................................................................ 87

My Ancestors Keep Me Up At Night .................................. 91

Beeps, and Bongs, and Chimes, Oh My! ............................. 94

Tim Tation ................................................................................ 96

**Empty Nesting .................................................................... 99**

Controlling What is Easy ..................................................... 100

Miracle of the Condiments ................................................. 102

And Then There Were None .............................................. 104

Snow Day Monopoly ...................................................................108

Bedspread Mountain....................................................................111

Parents Can Fly Too....................................................................114

**Mom's Wisdom**................................................................**117**

A Surprising Memory Aid .......................................................118

Fish and Company......................................................................120

I Just Realized I'm Old..............................................................124

Techno Granny ...........................................................................126

Cursing Through the Alphabet ..............................................129

**The Hands of Time**........................................................**131**

Laying Out....................................................................................132

I Cry at Everything ...................................................................136

Whose Hands Are on My Keyboard?....................................138

Crow's Feet, Chicken Arms, and Turkey Necks, .............141

There's a Babe Under There ..................................................144

Just Because I Used to Could, Doesn't Mean I Should.146

**Acknowledgements**........................................................**149**

**About the Author**............................................................**152**

## Why Did I Write This Book?

Because for as long as I could hold a crayon, pencil, or pen, I've been writing; I've been noting, jotting, and mostly journaling. This compulsion accelerated in childhood when I couldn't turn my bedside lamp off and go to sleep until I'd written in my flowery, fabric-covered Five Year Diary. I called the diary Denni, also the name of my long-distance pen pal I never met face-to-face. "Dear Denni..." It could be scary to think that my family's and friends' entire lives are ready-made for a documentary. Don't worry people, I'll never tell.

*Because* I have chronicled our children's lives in embarrassing detail, even before their births. I don't trust my memory and my five senses to record every day properly in my brain, so in true OCD fashion I've consolidated our lives on paper or on hard drives.

*Because* I became a blogger, sharing our private lives with anyone interested enough to read online. People began to read my essays and ask, "So when are you going to write a book?" After hearing that flattering question repeated, I decided that backing up life in book form was the next logical step. Everyone knows there's no such thing as too much backing up.

*Because* I want my mother to have something nice and clean, by her standards, to read. She is a speedy reader and will often read the ending of a book or scan for ugly language before wasting her time. If there are too many unsavory words, she'll write in pencil in the inside cover, "ugly," close the book and that's that. Into the giveaway pile it goes.

*Because* I want to embarrass my family and friends. Especially my kids. That's part of my job as a parent, a sister, a daughter, a pal. And if they fear what I might have written, they might actually read my writing. It's a win-win.

*Because* I'm not getting any younger. What if I write this book and people actually read part of it before storing it on the shelf with all their other partially read books? I might be inspired to write another. If you give a writer a compliment, they're gonna want another.

## Just Because I Used To Could

They're gonna keep on writing and maybe even publishing. So, if you don't want a writer to write, don't give them a compliment. It's like fudge to a chocoholic. Irresistible.

*Because* my bucket list is lame, I mean pretty much filled. I've checked most of the boxes thanks to my midlife status. I appreciate my life, the things I've done, the places I've been, and the people I know. I've recently checked off becoming a grandmother. His name is Wesley Jacob, after two of his great-grandfathers. That's a huge checkmark. One former bucket list item was to ride a horse on the beach. I scratched that one off the list when that dang horse named Mojo tossed me around like a sack of Vidalia onions while heading full-speed to the barn two hundred miles from the coast. There used to be places I'd like to visit on the list but if I don't get there, that's OK. Thanks to YouTube and the National Geographic Channel, I can visit Alaska with my dogs, from my own living room, while sipping coffee by the fireplace. I'm pretty sure *Write a Book* is the only item remaining on my list.

*Because* I have taken my own sweet time wondering if my G-rated humor was book-worthy and would have an audience. I decided time was a-wasting and to let the crazy ideas flow. Write the book already. I used to say, "Darn, I wish I'd written that!" Now, I can say, "Well dang if I didn't finally write it!"

# Healthy Living

## No Dairy, No Gluten, No Meat, Oh My!

I long to be known as a good home-cooking mom and grandmother, really, I do. I used to be a pretty bang up Southern cook who could whip up a banana pudding or potato salad in my grandmother's square yellow bowl and get a standing ovation. Well, huge accolades if not applause.

Not anymore. A few of our kids have so many restrictions in their diets that sometimes, it's hard to make my food taste better than cardboard. No dairy. No gluten. No meat. Oh my! Mindless eating and binging are a thing of the past in our house. Except when the kids aren't around. Then the hubs and I have a free-for-all of forbidden foods.

Granted, my kids have medical proof that they need dietary restrictions, but how am I supposed to maintain my cook extraordinaire title when I can't find a gluten-free replacement for Nilla Wafers that's worthy of my mama's banana pudding? And the pudding itself? Well, it contains dairy so there's that. Don't even get me started on the potato salad. I challenge anyone to come up with reasonable facsimile of a boiled egg for mama's special old-timey potato salad. Nine out of ten chickens agree, that's never gonna happen.

So, midlife arrived and I'm relearning to cook. Our oldest daughter, Danielle, had stomach issues for years, until finally, as an adult, she was diagnosed with Celiac Disease. Since then, she's been gluten-free, not by choice but by absolute necessity. At the beginning, we bought every gluten-free book available, spent an ungodly amount of money on special ingredients, and tried often in vain to create palatable food. Until you've tasted spelt, and other wheat alternatives, it's hard to appreciate America's amber waves of grain.

To avoid starvation or living off cardboard-tasting food, she finally got the hang of it and even married a guy who was mostly gluten-free as well. I'd rather eat their amazing cooking than mine, especially since I'm happy to be the eater and not the cooker. They continue to live happily ever after in their gluten-free home.

Our second daughter, Sarah, developed stomach issues and became not only gluten-free, but also vegan, which knocks out eggs and other dairy products. Wow. No eggs. I can't imagine an egg-free existence. Gluten-free can be done and vegan can be done, but putting them together moves cooking to a whole new dimension. She too taught herself to be a wonderful cook who can bake without a recipe. That is magical.

I get the vegetarian thing. I'm almost there myself. It must be all the videos I've seen of frolicking cows, sheep, and goats. And even snuggly pigs in doggie beds.

## Just Because I Used To Could

Soon, dancing birds will kill my taste for chicken nuggets.

Oh how I'd love to make my grandmother's chocolate pie packed with gluten and dairy the way she did. Well, actually I'd like someone else to make it since I'm not too thrilled about cooking anymore. I'd rather spend my time watching squirrels play, cats sleep, or nearly anything else. Even if I did make that special pie, I couldn't enjoy it. The guilt would eat me up, knowing my girls couldn't have any.

My solution is to have the young folks do most of the cooking. I say something like, "I could never make gluten-free pecan pie as good as yours," and my son-in law, Ben, who knows I'm talking about him, is in the kitchen, cranking out his famous pie.

"Show me how you make that chickpea, chicken-free chicken salad and that vegan macaroni and cashew cheese," I say to Sarah. These concoctions may sound odd to some, yet many a Southern cook can take strange ingredients whether by choice or due to limited resources and make a sumptuous, need-a-nap afterwards meal. When she demonstrates how to make these items work together, voila, there's a feast for all.

Welcoming creative cooks into the kitchen to create works of culinary art takes away all my guilt and kills two birds with that stone. Oh, sorry. Don't kill the bird. We're eating vegan/gluten-free tonight.

## Where are My Leg Warmers?

I remember the day my eighteen-year-old daughter, Sarah, asked me to exercise with her. I looked up from my paper-strewn desk where I was typing up a writing assignment, last minute as usual. "Who, me? Right now?"

"Yes, you. Take a break and let's use some of those old exercise videos you've kept since before I was born. The eighties are back, you know. You can show me some of your college disco moves. I need some exercise and a fun break from homework. Get up, woman. Let's do this."

How could I pass up my moment to shine? I'd memorized the routines on those videos many pounds and many years ago. I could show her my skills. And she thought it would be fun.

Well, it would have been fun if we could have convinced the massive, new TV to recognize the ancient VCR. The TV looked at me with a blank expression and said, "You want me to do what?" Well, really, it said nothing. It also did nothing.

Sarah, usually a techy with such things, tried all the remotes and setup buttons. She still couldn't make it

## Just Because I Used To Could

work even after slipping her tiny teenage self behind the TV cabinet and into the snake pit of cords and dust bunnies on the hardwood floor. Our aerobic workout was slipping away with each futile attempt to make the video play.

I told Sarah, "Look at this coffee table. We have at least four remotes and two game devices and neither one of us has any idea how to play a video of Richard Simmons, the dancercise king. Twenty years ago, we just needed one remote control with eight buttons: on, off, pause, play, fast-forward, reverse, record, and stop."

Disappointed but not defeated, we popped in a DVD of some young thing who smiled big and danced in her black yoga pants. Copying her hip-hop moves wasn't half as exhilarating as aerobicizing with Jane Fonda in her shiny neon workout gear, leg warmers, and Nike high-tops. I wanted Sarah to see me do the window-washing and drive-a-big-truck moves. I really hoped we could sweat to some oldies while Richard Simmons pranced in his little striped shorts, tank top, and headband.

Oh well. Sarah grinned at my serious lack of hip-hop skills. She really needs to see my aerobics moves. I can grapevine back and forth for hours and even add in a spin.

"We should see if Wal-Mart still sells a TV-VCR-DVD combo since our old one eats tapes like the deer eat our garden. And maybe we can pick up some leg warmers too. Mine are shoved somewhere in the attic alongside

Lisa Batten Kunkleman

my shimmery neon blue and pink leotards," I said with a wink.

## Something's Wrong with Chewing a Smoothie

If you have to chew your smoothie, it means you're a smoothie novice, not a smoothie king. The green concoction on my desk started out liquid, sort of. I'm not sure I want to finish off the healthy green blob in the bottom of my plastic tumbler. Maybe I added too much kale with the blueberries in my mad scientist attempt to make the ugliest cholesterol fixer-upper possible. Or perhaps the hemp and the chia seeds formed a Jell-O commune.

I think this ugly smoothie calls for a spoon. I try tilting the tumbler and the blob falls on my top lip and lands under my nose. Yuck! Who wants a green blob going up their nose? Drinking a strange potion can be difficult enough but even an ugly drink should be a liquid, not a solid.

I poke it with my straw and it's more solid than a Jell-O jiggler. I can't do it. It looks like something my cat leaves me for a gift. I'll make a fresh one for lunch or better yet, use a fork to eat my kale in a salad, topped with seeds, nuts, and my newest fun food, goji berries. That sure sounds more appetizing than chewing on a solid green smoothie that gives new meaning to a good solid meal.

## Sometimes Ugly is Good for You

*Dang, that's a good one.* Not long ago, while chewing my first smoothie, I knew something wasn't quite right. In a valiant attempt to regulate my cholesterol and triglycerides, I added a cartload of new foods to my diet. New, to me at least. Being Southern born and fed, I eat all kinds of greens, like collards, turnips, and kale, which lots of folks wouldn't touch for fifty bucks. Our family even grew them in our garden for a couple of decades. That was before new neighborhoods popped up, turning our farm into a deer cafeteria where they munch on our bountiful veggies, bushes, and weeds. I appreciate the weeding part.

    Several months ago, a nutritionist suggested I start drinking kale. I've allotted lots of fridge space to fresh fruits and veggies through the years, but it usually involved cooking and serving them on a plate or in a bowl. Now, I toss it all in my Oster blender, hit purée, and have a half-gallon of funky colored smoothie to graze on all morning. My blender, by the way, does a great job, so I've yet to invest in a five-hundred-dollar whopper-chopper. I spent oodles of money on a fancy juicer and that thing was harder to clean than the tracks of a sliding door. I sent it to a new forever home. I'll stick with my rinse-and-go blender till I burn out the motor.

    Lots of foods went into the blender this morning. Almond milk, kale, goji berries, oats, chia seeds, hemp, slivered almonds, a bunch of fruits, and some avocado. A year ago, I hardly knew some of these items were people food and now, my creations are pretty darn good. I'll keep fine-tuning my dump and blend method. I've already learned that a little more ice and water reduces the need to chew. My concoctions might be ugly, but they're my version of tasty energy drinks. When I was a kid, my grandparents had me drink the broth from the greens. They called it pot liquor and it was some kinda good. They'd probably be a little amused to know that like lots of folks nowadays, I'm drinking my kale.

# Body Wisdom

## Mammogram: Making the Most of It

Once again, it's time to check off all things medically necessary before the new insurance year begins. For me, that includes a mammogram. No problem. A simple phone call and a quick trip to the imaging center takes very little time and it's time well spent.

After checking in and a brief wait, hardly enough time to learn the latest about Brad and Angelina in the current *People* magazine, I hear my name called. A woman takes me back to the familiar little changing room closet with instructions to remove deodorant (wipes provided, of course), put on the pretty blue paper top with the snaps in front, and bring my purse with me to the private waiting room, where I may have coffee and snacks if I so desire.

I follow all the directions, including getting my cup of coffee. I also snap a couple of pictures of two bras on hangers decorated by some crafty soul to help increase awareness of breast cancer and the need for mammograms. One says, "Don't gamble with your life—Screening saves" and is decorated with playing cards, a roulette table and lottery tickets. The other says, "Nip breast cancer in the bud" and is decorated with silk flowers. Some people are so clever.

It's not my first encounter with that cold, hard machine and the technician's relaxed "I've seen more ta-tas than a *Playboy* photographer" attitude. "They're just another body part in a day's work."

She jokes around while placing my body parts in just the right position on the chilly tray for flattening. She might as well be imaging feet. We chat about life and the weather before she tells me, "You should get results in the mail in about two weeks. If you don't hear from us by Christmas, your letter's lost so give us a call."

No problem. I'll be done for another year unless I get a recheck call, which has happened twice. It's a little scary, but dense tissue and calcification can do that. Also, at the recheck appointment, they provide blue half gowns made of cloth instead of paper. A little more comforting for a woman whose chest might be quivering underneath that softer gown.

The technician tells me I'm getting the new 3-D imaging. When I made the appointment, the scheduler told me it costs an additional seventy-five dollars, not covered by my insurance. So worth it. Merry Christmas to me. I prefer no surprises from this office. I want to know everything.

Once imaging is complete, I step back into the little closet where my shirt and bra await, and I close the louvered door. I spot the deodorant provided and spray my right armpit. A familiar smell hits my nose, causing

## Just Because I Used To Could

me to read the bottle in my hand. Yep. Hairspray. Of course it is. Looking down I see a second spray bottle and pick it up. Yep. Antiperspirant. Of course it is.

I reach for a wipe and see there's not one sticking out of the box top. Of course not. I pick up the plastic container, dig down into the box and hit moisture. Yes! More wipes. I retrieve one and wipe my sticky underarm before the hairspray sets. Before I spray with the real antiperspirant, I read the bottle again for reassurance. And then, I use the hair spray...on my hair this time.

Deodorized and dressed, I take pictures of my tiny dressing room closet to remind me in the future to look before spraying. I fold my paper shirt and roll it up tight before stuffing it into my purse. I used to bring them to my kids to play dress-up but now, I use them for an occasional messy job or to protect my good clothes from a spaghetti meal. Don't judge. I'm not the first person to swipe a blue apron/bib/fashion statement and use free hairspray even if I don't need it. After all, I may as well get the most I can out of the mammogram experience.

## I'd Like to Change "The Change"

Why do women get to experience so much change in life? I'm referring to "The Change." I've long passed the age where I find change fun and exciting. There may be some spontaneity left in this old girl, but never knowing when my insides will boil and my face will turn red and bead with sweat is not my kind of living on the edge. Cooking from the inside out may be OK for a Crock-pot but not for a woman.

The title "The Old Crone" used to sound funny before I became one, an irritable wretch for two minutes per hour. That's two times twenty-four. That's forty-eight minutes a day that I'm a fiery, untouchable, hot ball of walking lava. Researchers say during a flash, my thermometer may say 98.6 but my skin temperature can rise from 5 to 7 degrees above that. If the thermometer registered that number, around 103 to 105, I'd be hospitalized. Thank goodness the body says, "What the heck? Let's turn off the heat," and "Finally I need a sweater." How can this happen to nice, peace-loving women like me?

My husband, Dan, who, bless his heart, sleeps with my feet in his face at various times every night, told me this morning, "You're burning up." He feels a flash coming on before I do if I've snuggled up to him in our heavily blanketed bed.

Heavily blanketed sounds counterproductive I know, but I peel them off like Pillsbury flaky canned biscuit layers as my personal global warming comes across in waves. Take off the top cozy spread, then the brown fleece blanket, then the sheet and I'm free to flip my head to the end of our California King bed so my face is directly under the ceiling fan. Poor, heat-loving Dan wakes up less than cozy with the ceiling fan swirling overhead as it does every night, all four seasons.

Out of habit, he might risk his life rubbing my feet as I cool off. It's a wonder he hasn't had black eyes and bloody noses for all the times I've kicked my feet and groused, "Puleeze don't touch me. I'm trying to cool off here. And stop flapping my pajama legs. That doesn't help get cool air up there."

I often stomp off to the blue-tiled bathroom where I splash cold water on my face and neck, feeling my already wet skin and hair become wetter. In the mirror, I look sunburned, bloated, and blotchy.

The cold water does nothing but make me soppier than I was, but it gets me out of the smothering bed that touches one whole side of my frying body. Standing upright in front of the ever-present little purple fan on my dresser allows air to circulate on my whole self except for the bottom of my feet. I know people who install heated floors. I'm thinking about converting half of my walk-in closet to a walk-in freezer.

As I'm returning to the bed, Dan says something nice like, "Are you ready to come back up here, right side up?"

"Lord what's wrong with you? No, I don't want to go back up there where you'll roast me like a marshmallow."

Knowing from his silent response that I was evil to Saint Dan, I crawl back into bed, head beside his. In mere moments I feel a chill and pull up the sheet, the fleece blanket, and the cozy top comforter. I nestle into my husband's toasty body and we fit like spoons.

"It's really cold in here," I say, pulling his arm around me and lacing my fingers with his.

## Blame My Muffin Top

I recently heard that belly fat, or as it is lovingly called, a muffin top, is actually a repository for wisdom and memories we don't often use. When the cauliflower-sized brain in our head gets filled up, all that reserve must go somewhere. I can totally believe in the muffin-belly storage compartment theory, but looking around I'm pretty sure some ladies who are missing a muffin top may have tush wisdom. We all have something.

If we believe this theory, we can take comfort in both our forgetting and our padding. The way I see it, our waists are a little ways down so it takes a while to pull data all the way up to the memory bank in our heads. For example, as I pointed my Honda key fob at the front door and didn't hear a click, I blamed my muffin top. Of course, I knew that key fob wouldn't work, but I had what some would call a senior moment. Since I'm not really all that much of a senior, just past the halfway mark, I chose to blame my muffin top. I used the same reasoning when I started to put the ice cream in the fridge, not the freezer. Darn muffin.

The other day, I was fetching the dirty clothes

hamper when my husband said from the shower, "I've already gathered the trash and recycling and it's sitting in the hall. If you want to set them on the porch, I'll take it all down the driveway in a few minutes."

I walked to the front door and set two containers on the porch. After loading the dishwasher with the morning minutiae, I headed for the laundry room to get a load of towels started. The whirr of the washer and dryer make great white noise for writing or at least that's what I like to think. Plus, the multitasking of doing laundry and writing feels very productive. Oddly, there was no laundry hamper to unload although I had just gathered all the stinky gym clothes from the kids' floors. I retraced my steps, walking through the foyer, and found the recycling container. I peeked out the front door and saw a can of trash and a blue laundry hamper overflowing with boy clothes. Muffin top.

Now I know why I forgot to pick up my sons from a Halloween party while I sat playing cards with my oldest daughter. Realizing I was two hours late retrieving them, I knew I'd blown my chance at mother of the year, yet again. After apologizing and entering the party-trashed home, I saw one of my forgotten eight-year-olds asleep on the birthday boy's sofa and the other was telling the boy's mom, "No I don't want this food. I'll wait to eat real food when I get home." Well, my child may not have used good manners but at least he thinks I'm a good enough mom to provide him with real food even if I did forget him. It's the muffin top's fault.

## Just Because I Used To Could

Should I apply the muffin-top-memory theory to the time I dropped off our preacher's daughter at her house and also left my son Joe behind? He had gotten out to visit their Labrador Retriever. I didn't even know he was missing till the daughter called to ask, "Miss Lisa, did you forget something?"

Calling people by their name is another issue I blame on my midsection. That one is major though, so I also throw in more realistic excuses like, "I'm so sorry, this *menopause/change of life thing* is really affecting my recall. Lately, I can't find my words." Or, "Sorry, the doctor has me on migraine meds that make it hard for me to think." People don't look at me like I have three heads if I tell them that. Both of those excuses are true, but I still believe there's something to the muffin theory.

And there's always the water hose left filling the horse trough for twelve hours and the spaghetti water boiling out, so the bottom of the pot was welded to the stove eye. Definitely the muffin top's fault, because my cauliflower of a brain must be completely full.

Need I go on? I hope other women take comfort knowing there's a real excuse for our forgetting. So, laugh off those senior moments for now and embrace that muffin top. Blame it for everything. Enjoy that padding and just forget about your newfound forgetfulness.

## Cicadas in My Head

My friends Marcie, Linwood, and I stood under a street light in the foggy parking lot of the Cumberland County Memorial Arena in Fayetteville, North Carolina. We were waiting for Linwood's dad to pick us up for our hour-long ride back to our homes in Whiteville. Brand new teens, we'd been rocking out to our favorite band, Grand Funk Railroad, with prime tickets on the arena floor. Still exhilarated from attending our first real concert, we laughed about our ringing ears. We found it funny, sort of like a helium voice, although we knew it wasn't normal.

"Y'all sound like you're talking through a glass door. I can see your mouths moving but I can barely hear you," I shouted.

"I know. Same with me," yelled Marcie.

What seemed funny to us at the time wasn't so humorous after all. Standing smashed in the crowd so close to the stage might have been amazing but it also meant being too close to the ginormous bank of speakers.

Decades later, my head humming in a monotone, it's not so amusing. When I can hear the music young people are jamming to with their ear buds in, I have to force myself not to yank their cords and give them a mama lecture. Hopefully we won't have a whole new generation with ringing ears. It's called tinnitus, but I call it "cicadas in the head."

That temporarily entertaining feeling in youth lost its hilarity long ago with my own personal teapot whistling and whirring in my ears. It's like having a head full of buzzing bugs. I can usually ignore the incessant sounds during busy daytime hours but at nighttime, the marsh inside my head comes alive.

I have discovered a helpful solution. Opening our rural bedroom window adds additional critters and harmony to the bug symphony. I throw in the not-so-distant highway sounds. I pretend the 18-wheelers are ocean waves and the screaming motorcycles are jet skis that are jumping those waves. My nights are filled with orchestras, swamps, and oceans, as I lie back and ride those sound waves to dreamland.

## Patent Pending

I need an orthopedist and an immobilizing boot. Doesn't everybody? It's the thing to do these days, at least at our house. We injure bones and joints, causing limps and groans. We get X-rays and MRI's that lead to steroids and physical therapy. We elevate and ice, heat and wrap.

We've spent so much time and money on our local bone doctors, they should hang an *In Honor of...* plaque with our names engraved on it, and we're not alone. Exercise and sports injuries are rampant. Torn ACL's. Knee replacements. Bunion-ectomies. Hip replacements.

These days, so many people wear immobilizing boots, they're becoming a fashion statement. They certainly cost enough to be fashionable and serve as instant conversation starters. It's almost as good as walking a cute dog, which according to my dad is how he got my mom to first notice him.

After a recent immobilizing boot encounter, I should be on a first name basis with the guy in front of me at the grocery store. We started talking and learned far too much not to know each other's names.

"Oh, look! We're twins." The stranger in the

grocery line looked up from his phone and smiled as I pointed at his big black immobilizing boot.

"So, how'd you get yours?" I asked.

"Chasing my dog around to get my new running shoe out of his mouth. He's a digger so our yard's like an obstacle course. And you?"

"It's a nerve injury called Morton's Neuroma, from stepping off a curb wrong. I ignored the pain until an all-day Thanksgiving cooking marathon did me in. I could hardly walk the next morning. Plus, Plantar Fasciitis in my heels and Metatarsalgia in the balls of my feet like I've had before. It feels like walking on pebbles. Don't you just love throwing out medical terminology? I bet you know your share of fancy words, too."

The stranger nodded. "Oh yeah. I'm practically a doctor now. I had Plantar Fasciitis a while back. Felt like walking on broken glass. My physical therapist had me freezing ice in a Styrofoam cup, and then tearing the bottom off the cup to rub the ice on my aching heels. My wife wasn't thrilled about my cold, drippy puddles on the sofa. It's a real fracture this time."

"Check out this picture of how massive and colorful it was at first," he said.

"Wowza." I looked at his pictures before pulling up my own. "Your swollen, purple mass looks a lot like mine," I said.

"Yep. Twins," he said, pocketing his phone and handing his milk and eggs to the checkout clerk.

"Nothing like the musical sounds of Velcro straps

and boot clunk. But I don't have to tell you how annoying all that Velcro can be," I said, pushing my cart forward.

"Nope. I'm a boot expert now," the stranger said as he picked up his bagged groceries to leave. "Good luck."

"You too. Yeah, someone should go into the boot business. Add some color, and logos, maybe even fur trim. I'll start working on that," I said.

"Ha. I might just do that myself. See who gets them on the market first. Have a good one," he said.

I dreamed of designer orthopedic boots that night. Four friends and I were on a runway modeling our new line of upscale immobilizing boots. Red for Christmas and Valentine's. A two-in-one bargain. Silver for New Years and white for winter. Pastels for spring and Easter egg colors. Patriotic of course for July 4$^{th}$. Orange for Halloween. Pilgrim buckles on brown leather for Thanksgiving.

I woke up wide-eyed and inspired to start a business. My parents and grandparents were all in the shoe business so perhaps it was my pre-ordained destiny. Immobilizing boots are pricey enough in basic black but what if Uggs wanted in on the deal. Could this be our foot in the door of wealth? Our family alone could be the spokespersons, since my kids and I take turns wearing them anyway.

Afterthought: I velcroed all my aggravating boot straps and was so exhausted, I decided someone else could take my dream and go for it, with my blessing.

## Another Thing My Knees Don't Like

Well shoot! Another thing my knees don't like. Tennis. That's the only land-sport I've ever had the potential for being OK at. Nowadays every time I hit a few balls my joints crunch and scream at me for the next few weeks. Sorry, tennis. You're not worth it.

I know people who are getting replacement parts—knees, shoulders, hips, teeth, and all kinds of parts. I, on the other hand, have had more than enough surgeries in my long quest for a large family. I'm pretty much done with the operating room.

I've chosen to give up some of the things I *used-to-could* do and instead pick up some new activities that don't involve joint noise and strain. For instance, I love water sports but the last time I tried to ski, my crouch position became my cannonball position where the boat dragged me a few yards before the rope pinged away from my hands. OK. Done with that. Check it off the list of things I *used-to-could but that doesn't mean I should*. I'll be just fine lazing around on a fancy new float, thank you very much.

While we're on the subject of skiing...snow skiing is on that list. While I was never very good, I did enjoy a sloppy swoop down a mountain now and then. The last time was more scary than sloppy as I lived in constant fear of hurting my precious knees. I checked that off the *used-to-could* list. Good riddance. I'd rather sit in the lodge by the fire, drink coffee and read, and write. There's plenty of story material with the oodles of church youth groups clomping around in ski boots and braving the stage to sing karaoke that is not exactly microphone worthy. They all deserve applause for bravery if not for talent.

And then there's squatting. I spent most of my younger years squatting and bunny-hopping up from that squat position while my mother would say, "I used to do that. Not anymore. The knees can't take it." I know the feeling, Mom. A car wreck in the '70s and High Impact Step Aerobics in the '80s may have started the knee grind, but getting bucked off a horse named Mojo moved my meniscus and the crunch to a whole new octave. I can live with the noise, but I sure do miss my squat. I miss gardening the most. I still do it but it's not a pretty sight. Having to get on all fours to plant and weed, and then push my tall self back up straight to standing position, somehow it's just not the same.

Now, on the bright side, as long as I treat these knees right, meaning no jumping, squatting, twisting, standing up on water behind a boat or on a slippery slope, I'm just fine. And that's not bad for these middle-aged knees that are my original set. I hope to keep it that way.

# Nature is Never Boring

## Bullying or Flirting?

Horses: How can you tell if animal behavior is good or bad? While I was out of town, my man Dan sent me a short video of our male horse harassing our mare. When I got home, Dan called me outside to see our equine bully in action. I marched out to where Titan, our white-faced gelding, was biting our beautiful reddish-brown mare, Sassy, on her backside. I shouted "No!" and "Stop it, Titan!"

He gave me a puzzled look and started to nip her again. I called Titan to me at the fence. He let me rub his nose and give him a kiss, then moments later he put his head over the fence and tried to bite my hand. I'm not into yelling or physical punishment but through shock and instinct I swatted his nose and scolded him again.

Dan joined me at the fence and asked me if this new wild side could be mating behavior. I was thinking the same thing. Even though Titan had been "fixed" long ago, perhaps his libido was still intact.

Naturally, I googled *Mating behavior in horses*, and *Can a gelding still mate?* Oh my, the number of answers was vast and decisive. In a word, "Yes," all his symptoms met the criteria for a male, gelding or not, having a strong sense of smell and desire for a female in season. He sure was sniffing her mare perfume all over her neck and rear quarters.

I felt guilty for yelling at Titan and yet, I felt sorry for Sassy, an older woman with bad knees, getting her hiney bitten repeatedly. Surely, she wasn't enjoying his overzealous attention. But who am I to know about horse flirting?

Having two mares in the past, this was never an issue. They only fought over food and human attention. I guess Titan is like most males who act stupid around a "sexy" woman. I'd never thought of our girl Sassy as a hot mama. Funny, I now realize Sassy did lots of tail lifting that I attributed to releasing nervous gas instead of being an attempt at seduction and saying, "Hey, big fellow."

Dogs: The horses aren't the only confusing species. There's our hyperactive granddog, Charlie the Vizsla, a handsome tank that could mow down a whole canine football team when he's at full speed. He's a licking machine, lover of people and pets, and sometimes a personal space invader. Sadie, our big black and tan coonhound, hides when her doggie nephew comes over. He's all about the licking and wrestling.

While dog-sitting Charlie, I was pleased to see the big puppy being gentler with our three dogs, which we call his aunts and uncle. I even recorded his good behavior on my phone. It was so cute. He licked our Sadie hound's jowl and lay his head across her body like a snuggle. He even sniffed our boy Sheltie Remy's rear quarters. Remy showed his teeth, ready to teach him who's the king of this castle. Charlie moved on to our passive Border Collie/St. Bernard mix, Mandy. He nuzzled her without biting and pulling the fur off her fuzzy ears. That was a first.

While Mandy lay on the fireplace rug, Charlie stood over her; he placed his head and front paws across Mandy's neck and wallowed all over her like a happy pig in mud, as she pretended to sleep. He appeared to be swimming in her gorgeous long fur. Finally, Charlie snuggled his long, copper body up to her and rested his head on her fluffy back. They slept. I was so happy to catch this momentous occasion on video. All of us have used Mandy's soft body for a pillow at one time or another.

When my daughter came to fetch Charlie, I showed her the video, knowing she'd be pleased that he was not roughing up her fur siblings. She watched for a minute and said, "Mom, I can't watch this. This is not sweet behavior. It's dominant behavior. Don't let him do that to Mandy. He's being a bully."

Well pooh! So, after decades of parenting animals, I can't get it right. I think romantic advances in horses are bullying, and I think bullying dominance in dogs is romantic and sweet. I wonder if my judgment is off in lots of other things. Am I this mixed up about human behavior as well? I've got some pondering to do.

## You Swim with What?

"How can you swim in a lake that has alligators?"

I hear that all the time. I can't really explain it without sounding crazy, but I'll just say, "Go there just once and you'll understand." Lake Waccamaw gets into a person's heart and is difficult to push out of there.

I myself am deathly afraid of gators and feel more comfortable seeing where they are than wondering. I enjoy watching them lounge around on the bank of the canal adjacent to the swamp on a sunny day. Would I enjoy watching one lounge in our yard? Heck no! Do I relish seeing one's long snout floating anywhere near our area of the lake? Oh no. Heck no!

I remember once, decades ago when I spotted a

long, bumpy black nose between our pier and the neighbor's, about twenty feet from shore. I called the wildlife department and asked if someone could remove our visitor which should go back to the swamp.

The man on the phone, obviously locally born and bred if his slow drawl was an indication, said, 'Ma'am, these gators was here long before we came, and they'll be here long after we're gone." He laughed. "Just leave 'im alone and he'll get on outa there when he's ready."

I did. Leave him alone. The family and I tired of watching him just lie there with his snout in the air. We decided to drive around the lake and have lunch at Dale's Seafood while we waited out Wally Gator's departure. Sure enough, when we came back, he was gone. We spent several hours standing on the pier, staring down and all around into the clear, tea-colored water, checking out the shallow sandy bottom. Once the all clear was announced, everyone was back in the water splashing and squealing enough to run off any peace-loving gator.

We don't see them in the lake all that often. They mostly stay in the swamp and the canal, perhaps not wanting a passing boat or skier to whack them in the head. I can name most of the times they've been seen at the surface. Of course, I can't name all the times they've been holding their breath, lurking unseen beneath the water. That's the part that unnerves me. But not enough to keep me from swimming.

## Where Did All the Gators Go?

Fear of gators doesn't stop my husband from paddle boarding to and from the grasses near the dam at Lake Waccamaw when the water is calm. One day he glided up to our pier saying, "I met a gator this morning."

"Oh my gosh, how close? And what did you do?" I asked.

"Not too far from me. I just eased inland a little and kept on balancing and kept on paddling," he said, as if it was just another morning paddle and he'd met a duck.

Hightailing it for home or at least somebody's pier is more like it. He pretended it didn't faze him, but I'm sure he either said some big old words or some big old prayers for good balance and speed.

Killing a gator in North Carolina is still a colossal no-no, even after they were cut from the endangered species list as of 1987. Thanks to gator protection under the Endangered Species Act of 1973, their population is booming. Let's just say, there are mixed reviews about their boom being a good or a bad thing. People either like the cool factor of having prehistoric creatures hanging around, or they don't like it one little bit. It reminds me of people debating "The only good snake is a really dead snake" versus "Snakes keep our varmint population under control."

Some folks really want to have a hunting season with a special one-gator-per-hunter permit, and the idea almost passed through legal hurdles when another idea postponed that proposal. A scientific approach to study the gators would happen first. As I understand it, scientists tagged about seventy-some gators in the summer of 2018 to check out their lifestyle and migration patterns. Do they stay in one area or are they moving around from swamp bank to swamp bank? Inquiring minds want to know.

Soon after the tagging was finished, Hurricane Florence and Hurricane Michael pounded the East coast and flooded the area so deeply that the swamps, canals, yards, and the lake joined to become one massive body of water. Our red barn house looked like an island in the water, as did all the other houses in the area. Wonder where all those tagged gators floated off to in all that water? People found yards and ditches full of stranded fish when the water receded, but the walking water creatures wandered off somewhere and survived. Where? I'd like to think the critters wanted to retreat back to their lairs, to get back to home sweet home, but I'm not that naïve. Many of them probably liked their new digs and decided to float around for a while. Until we get the scientists' reports back, I suppose folks will keep on watching and wondering, where did all the gators go?

## Stray-Dar

It can't be a coincidence that four of our animals found us at Lake Waccamaw in Columbus County, North Carolina. It's not like we lived there year-round. Animal genes must be extraordinary in that small county since they're able to sniff out soft-hearted humans from miles away.

Our family spent as much time as possible at our parents' red barn-shaped cabin on Lake Waccamaw, North Carolina's best-kept secret. Each of those animals managed to show up and connect with us at just the right time during our visits to the lake, despite the fact that we live in Charlotte about three hours away.

**Boo Boo:** First there was Boo Boo, a shaggy dog rescued from the local animal shelter by our neighbor Patsy, who was seeking a boxer. Patsy saw beneath the matted, muddy mutt's exterior a wonderful dog and brought him home. Once she cleaned him up and got him vet checked, she learned that Boo Boo had heartworms. Not a good diagnosis—difficult and expensive to treat.

The day my eyes met Boo Boo's bushy bangs, it was love. He looked like a Soft Coated Wheaten Terrier mix. A purebred would have been worth a pretty penny, but who cared about that? He was adorable. I told Patsy I'd always wanted a shaggy dog like him so if she decided to keep looking for a Boxer, I'd take him. She discussed it with her husband who was already growing attached to the sweet dog, and they agreed to let Boo Boo join our family. Oh happy day. I had my shaggy dream dog. Treating heartworms was no picnic for him, or us, but he was well worth it.

What a dog. He was the first dog ever living inside the house. Due to his precarious heartworm treatment, he had to be calm and still, with no running or jumping for three months. That was a challenge. Boo Boo was the beginning of our house going to the dogs, and cats. Literally. A menagerie of accidents, fur, and nibbled furniture. Over the decades our poor animal house has seen it all.

Just Because I Used To Could

**Mandy**: Patsy once again visited the animal shelter, this time with her granddaughter, Natalie. The two of them brought home a little brown and white fur ball with a 'possum tail. No fur on that tail at all. She was in a cage labeled Pit Bull. Ha. She looked more like a lop-eared bunny and a 'possum mix than a Pit Bull.

One visit next door to see the new puppy and our kids were smitten, saying they wished we could have a puppy. I reminded them we had plenty of pets with a sitter awaiting our arrival back home. Everyone was pretty much pacified until Natalie's mom came to fetch her and said, "I'm sorry, Nat. We cannot have another dog. I think nine is plenty." They raised long-haired Chihuahuas at the time. Let the waterworks begin. Natalie and our triplets, ten years old at the time, brought the fur ball onto our screen porch. The kids' faces were as long as a hound dog's and they all whimpered and whined at once:

"Mom says I can't keep her," said Natalie.

"She can't go back to the pound," said one of mine.

"Tomorrow's kill day," said Natalie.

"Mom, we can't let her go back," said one of mine.

On and on it went.

Finally, I said, "We can't keep her, but we'll try to find her a home. Do you remember how hard it was to find a pet sitter for our menagerie just to come down to the lake for a week? We can't add any more."

The first step to giving in was a local vet visit to learn that the puppy, already named Mandy by Natalie, had ringworm and that's why she had a possum tail.

"Bathe her in sulfur for several weeks and she'll be fine. It's the people around her catching ringworm that's the problem..." said the veterinarian. Just the words I dreamed of hearing. Who would want a puppy with ringworm? I knew we were done for. She had her new family. Resisting the expression in those big ol' eyes was ridiculous. Mandy was Lake Waccamaw pet number two.

**Daisy Mae**: "What the heck is that? There's something black running around under the porch!" The kids were all butts-up-in-the-air with heads under the screen porch. Yep. The same lake house. I have no memory of who caught the kitten or how, but once again, there was a homeless pet on the screen porch and lots of pleading eyes aimed in my direction.

This time, it was my husband who was smitten with the kitten, which sealed that deal. She became Daisy Mae. Our gorgeous, persnickety cat that may bless you with her presence if she decides you are worthy. Getting to touch her luxurious fur is like receiving knighthood from the queen. Something you don't soon forget.

**Sadie Mae**: And then along came Sadie Mae. While cutting bushes outside the same lake house, a starving stranger arrived in the yard. She snuck up on my future son-in-law Ben and in his words, "She asked for a turkey sandwich." Sadie, all skin, ribs, and enormous eyes, appeared to be a black and tan coonhound.

Just Because I Used To Could

A hunting dog that must not have been very good at her job. There's no telling how long that dog had been wandering around the swamp. She was too skinny even for a gator to be interested, yet, as emaciated as she was, Sadie looked like royalty riding in the back seat of our van on the way to the vet. Yep, another vet trip during our vacation.

She filled out fast and gobbled down her food even faster, because once a starved animal, always a starved animal. Sadie was our gorgeous hound that made her presence known by tapping her feet and spinning in circles for food. She shared her hound scent and blessed us with her hound howl. We called her Single Stare Sadie because she could stare any of us down making us want to feed her another turkey sandwich. Now that was one special dog.

After that familiar eleven-mile trip to the vet in Whiteville, we had our fourth Columbus County animal. Each one was a treasure. Rescued animals are mighty special. We're down to two dogs, a cat, and two horses. That's not many for us. It wouldn't surprise me if another animal finds us before long during one of our Lake Waccamaw visits. They smell us coming from miles away.

## Rake the Lake

Few people know the joys of Lake Waccamaw, North Carolina. That's not all bad, either. We're not really selfish people but we do tend to keep the lake in the category of Best Kept Secrets. Despite the fact that I hear myself expounding upon the alligator population and the aquatic vegetation, hydrilla, taking over the lake, I wonder if I'm trying to keep our natural treasure all to ourselves.

Several times a year, Lake Waccamaw is well publicized and people come from all directions to join in the festivities like rodeos and a Farm Days Festival on the grounds of the Boys and Girls Home.

Independence Day is a popular holiday at the lake. July 4th fireworks circle the lake shoreline and

## Just Because I Used To Could

grow more outstanding every year. It's like having dozens of semi-professional shows in the middle of The Green Swamp. Mounds of fireworks boxes line the road on July 5th and show us exactly where the expert and novice pyro-technicians were producing their colorful performances.

Then there's Labor Day and the Take the Lake celebration. People prepare for months and even years to complete the Personal Endurance Challenges offered, which include walking/running/hiking/biking around the lake and for the water savvy folks, paddling the fourteen miles of shoreline and/or swimming across the four-mile body of water. Finally, there are the super athletes we all admire who attempt or accomplish the Take the Lake Extreme to complete all of the above: walk/run, paddle, bike/hike, and swim. They are the closest we have to great Olympians in Columbus County.

Back in 2011, at our house on Waccamaw Shores, we developed a third event that we think needs publicity for all of us on Lake Time. We named it Rake the Lake. All summer, the tickly green, grassy stuff some called an algae-bloom-gone-wild was growing in the sandy bottom of the lake. Swimming through the jungle of growth was not helping our breaststrokes at all.

Then along came Hurricane Irene. Her waves helped loosen the plants and the green stuff became floating blobs of vegetation. While we were happy to see the sandy bottom again, swimming into the floating garden often meant coming up for air and realizing you had a slimy green hitchhiker on your head.

The vines clogged up our jet skis after sucking the greenery underneath into the filter-thingy my husband calls an intake grate. Skiing became a new kind of obstacle course as skiers tried to dodge the tangles of gunk or at least not fall into a green nest.

While athletes kayaked and swam by our pier, we were standing on the shoreline of the normally clear water, pulling out huge clumps of green, hairy-looking goo. Through a stroke of genius, our family and some of our neighbors took rakes into the lake and just as a pool gets skimmed, the lake got raked. Piles of green gunk grew tall on our piers and along the shoreline as it was scooped and tossed pitchfork-style up and out of the water. The mountains of grassiness became taller than our heads, so we had some great Kodak moments. After umpteen wheelbarrow loads were piled at the roadside, our small section of lake was completely clear. We could see our feet and not be trapped by slimy green tentacles. Several neighbors raked their part of the lake and their waterfronts were pristine too.

After seeing and smelling the difference with the odiferous piles gone, I proposed in an article in the local newspaper, *The News Reporter*, that others might want to follow suit. It wasn't a perfect solution to the green gunk collection, but it certainly couldn't hurt. We thought of it like dusting. The dust may come back but at least you have a feeling of clean for a little while. Also,

## Just Because I Used To Could

raking the lake was terrific aerobic activity with some weight training included. Perhaps Rake the Lake could be considered physical training for Take the Lake if we have another plant invasion.

## Winged Invasion

What do you call millions of mayflies swooping in and covering your house, boat, cars, and ground? Annoying? Ridiculous? I call it a plague. When these two-inch-long cousins of the dragonfly swarm in, there's nothing to do but watch in amazement.

They covered our family cabin at Lake Waccamaw, North Carolina, with the speed of a Boston blizzard. Only it's a blizzard of bugs. Within minutes, the siding of our barn-shaped house, the porch floor and rails, and the bushes nearby were encased with the critters. Our red house turned tan and the porch railing was almost pretty, adorned with living ruffles. They reminded me of synchronized swimmers with their wings all facing the same direction, or maybe more like a carpet of faded out fairies at a convention.

Strange as it may sound to entomophobes—folks with a fear of insects—we didn't run back inside. How could we miss a surprise bug blizzard? We had a rough time sneaking out through the darker back screened porch to see what was happening without bugs getting in. Moments before, we were merely trying to walk the dog when, lo and behold, we saw dozens of the alien-

## Just Because I Used To Could

looking creatures with long antennae-like tails dotting the front storm door. There was no way to get back inside through the front door, fully encased by now.

By the time my niece, brother, and I closed our mouths to keep from munching a passing mayfly, the lawn and gravel drive were carpeted in a writhing and wiggling love fest in order to propagate their species. Others dangled on shrubbery like earrings.

My niece, already taking photos that could rival those in *National Geographic*, kept calling us over to look at one spectacle after another. We especially got a kick out of the little fellows riding around on our feet. I left the photography to her while I googled the life cycle of mayflies. Don't judge me. Yes, I stood there with bugs on the tops of my feet while I researched our tiny new arrivals. Apparently, mayflies rise from the lake bottom to the surface, fly into the air to mate, drop eggs back to the lake bottom, and fall breathless onto the water. There, they become a feast for the fish waiting below.

That's what's supposed to happen, but a strong wind that day must have blown them inland and they were confused. That's just my theory. Plus, we had lights on. I also learned that mayflies are drawn to light, which explains why they blessed us with their arrival. Houses all around us were dark, uninhabited at the time, so we won the insect jackpot.

My Google search revealed that in Pennsylvania, mayflies swarm to the lighted bridges, covering rails and the road, often piling up to six inches deep on bridges, causing car and motorcycle accidents. One source claims that driving on the bugs *en masse* is like driving on ice requiring the slippery critters to be removed with snowplows.

Squealing like little girls, we brushed the bugs from our hair. After taking another picture of them decorating our shoes, we stomped to get them off our ankles and feet, and made a run for the screened porch. As we squished through the carpet of bugs, still wearing a few mayfly ornaments on our ankles and shoes, we smelled a definite fishy odor. The odor makes perfect sense since they came from the bottom of a lake. We took off our shoes to find the bottoms covered in what looked like nutty brownie mix. So much for my new fancy flip-flops. An unfortunate casualty of the mayfly plague, they still reek of fish, so I'll only get to wear them at the beach. That is, as long as there are no hungry seagulls nearby. I've had enough winged creatures landing on my feet.

The morning after the infamous invasion shone new light on the final stage of the mayfly life cycle. The decorated house would soon be swept and washed clean of the remains. I felt a little melancholy for the bugs. What a cruddy life. They never eat a bite of food and only live a day or two. Their short life cycle seemed especially useless since they missed the lake and the fish wouldn't get their mayfly morsels this year. Experts say that lights draw them onto manmade surfaces. Hopefully they'll fulfill their purpose next spring; you better believe we'll shut off the porch lights.

## A Broom is My Snow Blower

We don't need a snow blower in Charlotte. We just need a broom, and perhaps to puff out our cheeks, pucker our lips, and blow. Our snow tends to be light and wispy, bordering on wishful thinking most of the time. With one of our typical snow events, we watched tiny flurries lift our hopes for a moment before dashing them mere moments later, the snow clouds morphing into a photo-worthy sunset.

Now, ice is a different matter. North Carolinians know how to have an ice storm and are masters of the milk and bread grocery store dash in preparation for those famous milk sandwiches referred to in a tired Southern joke. We also clear the shelves of rock salt, batteries, snow shovels, sleds, and shredded cheese. Sorry, I doubled back to the dairy aisle for that last item.

The city closes for good reason. Roads shouldn't be used to play bumper cars. Even if people claim they can drive in ice, don't believe it. Vehicles don't come equipped with skate blades or skis for tires, so they have no traction. I've yet to see a car angle its tires in a *V* and *pizza* to a stop like a bunny slope skier.

In the interest of safety and keeping the streets

clear for emergency vehicles, people are encouraged to stay home when ice storms hit our city. People make fun of the South closing down for our tiny spritz of frozen stuff, but trust me, we're better off avoiding the road if possible. Without enough equipment to clear snow-covered asphalt, dealing with wrecked cars scattered about on the ice is an insurmountable task.

Power can be a real bugger in ice storms. As a designated Tree City, USA, once our ample tree canopy is slathered in ice, the weight of the limbs falling across the above ground electric lines often causes extensive power outages. Our family has an additional issue to deal with when ice storms hit. Our farm, nestled in suburbia, still runs on well water, which requires electricity to pump the water up and into the house. That means if our power goes out, we have don't have electricity or water. It's like living in The Little House on the Prairie. At the first threat of an ice storm, our family knows the steps to take in order to be prepared.

1. Hoard some $H_2O$: We might look like overly zealous survivalists hoarding jugs or large pots of water in our guest bathtub for drinking and hygiene, plus filling our extra horse trough so we can flush toilets if the power goes out, but experience is an excellent teacher. We've gone without water enough to know it is no fun. With a full house, being prepared is a good thing. Just in case. If we don't need that reserved $H_2O$, it can be

used later for pasta and tea, and the horses have plenty to drink.
2. Snag a shower: Nobody wants to get stuck feeling gross and flat-headed for several days if there's no water, and you sure don't want to wash your hair in the ice-cold liquid stashed in jugs in the guest bathtub. So, everybody takes a shower even if they recently took one or will take one in a few hours if by some miracle the power stays on. We do it. Just in case.
3. Protect precious pipes: When record lows threaten single-digit cold weather, we put a fresh light bulb in the uninsulated pump house to keep the well pump nice and cozy, so it won't freeze. We also let all the faucets drip and pray the pipes don't freeze and burst. Who needs that?

Our winter weather is nothing compared to the Northeast, the Midwest, or even the mountains of North Carolina where most of our kids have lived and now know what really cold means. I hear it's thirty below in Wisconsin, and school is in session. We have no reason to complain. We barely make the news unless our peach or strawberry crops are endangered, but this is Charlotte and another snow that didn't happen. We got sleet and ice instead. We were wishing for fatter flakes and snow cream, snowmen and sledding, at least at our house. Our snowstorm turned out to be nothing but a cold *cold front*. The kids had two days out of school without a snowman in sight. Hmmm... I hope nobody from up in the perpetually frozen north reads this.

## Eclipse Watching

Eclipse, eclipse, eclipse. That was sure a big story on the news. You'd think it was a rare occurrence or something. On our farm in Charlotte, North Carolina, crescent shadows shone everywhere. With no fancy eclipse glasses, of course we couldn't look up toward the sun and burn our retinas, so we looked down instead.

My husband had planned on using his dad's old welding helmet but one of our sons asked to borrow it since eclipse glasses were completely sold out except from price gougers. What are you gonna do? Let our son fry his eyes or burn our own? He took the helmet to college. That's why we were reduced to using a holey kitchen gadget and trees. Afterwards, he said the helmet didn't work as well as some girl's eclipse glasses he borrowed. Of course.

A scientist on the news advised looking through a colander or simply down at light between the leaves' shadows. I'd heard that another safe trick to see the eclipse was through the holes of a Ritz cracker, but we were fresh out. We did have some Chicken and Biscuit crackers but decided to eat them and try looking through colander holes instead.

We also tried using the hole in an old record album to check out the sun phenomenon on our cement driveway but that was boring. We wondered if the retina-damaging rays would warp a vinyl album. Hands down, nature's own colander of leaves worked the best, reflecting sickle-shapes everywhere beneath them. When the kids were little, sometimes we'd use chalk and outline shadows. With the kids away from our empty nest, I plum forgot to drag out the chalk to do eclipse shadow art.

We never went completely dark even though we were in the coveted eclipse path, and people drove across country to observe the rare event from our vantage point. It got dark enough for our horses to neigh but maybe it wasn't the darkness as much as seeing us outside and deciding it must be an early suppertime. The dogs wanted to sunbathe on the pavement, but I made them come back into the shade. They didn't understand that at all since they spend most days baking in the warm sun. Sadie Hound scared me by looking skyward when I called her name. Hopefully the sun didn't do any damage to her beautiful sad-sack peepers.

How many people will fear they've done something wrong to their own eyes by taking their special glasses off too soon or putting them on too late or sneaking a peak at the dangerous orb? How many people will go see an eye doctor just to be sure all is fine? My eyes feel a little irritated just thinking about it. I felt like a daredevil taking a selfie on my iPad with the sun behind

## Just Because I Used To Could

my back, photo-bombing my picture. ABC News said that was OK but I'm still not so sure. Maybe I'll see the ophthalmologist next week. It's about time for my annual eye check-up anyway. Ooo, I might get some new frames.

## A Bathtub Full of Hurricane Prep Water

What do you do with a bathtub full of water after the danger of hurricane force winds has passed? Do you pull the plug and watch it glug down the drain, serving absolutely no purpose except to give the pipes a little rinse?

No sir-ee. Not in our house. We learned an awful lot about rationing water when Hurricane Hugo crashed through Charlotte in 1989, leaving us powerless for nine long, hot days. In our case, relying on well water, no power means no water since it takes electricity to pump the well. After learning the hard way how important water is in day to day life, there's no way my husband Dan and I could ever let that much saved up water go down the drain without serving a purpose. I know it may sound silly, but surviving that hurricane in the '80s with just a few large pots of water to brush teeth and take birdbaths really stuck with us.

When Hurricane Michael threatened, we filled a bathtub and double-checked the plug after learning a hard lesson during Hugo. We filled a tub in preparation for Hurricane Hugo, like we were supposed to. If only we'd known the drain plug in our old powder-blue master bathroom tub had a slow leak, we might have actually had water to flush the potties or take a bath. That blue tub should have looked like a baby splash pool but instead looked like a dry pool drained in winter for repairs.

Once the threat of high winds and power outage passed, we left our daughter's lovely, late '60s purple ceramic bathtub full of water for about a week, knowing our dogs would soon need a bath. Call us crazy, but it was a good idea. Our daughter is away at school, meaning her tub sits unused most of the time and has a modern-day rubber stopper. We learned our lesson about leaky old tubs.

Bath day finally arrived so I washed the dingiest two of our three dogs. OK, the smelliest two. You could hardly see the purple under all that brown, dirty dog water. Their reaction was priceless. Neither of these two dogs is a fan of baths. But this time, they stepped over the side of the tub and into the foot-high water like it was a spa. How were we to know that all this time they've preferred a deep soak to wading up to their ankles and having pitchers of rinse water dumped on them? Maybe I'll find one of them snuggled up in that tub wishing someone with opposable thumbs would fill it for them to have another hot tub experience.

What can you do with a bathtub of water after a hurricane has passed? This question could apply to anything accumulated in excess that might get tossed without considering alternative uses. Ready to give up on those teeny tiny-waisted pants, the mounds of old magazines, and the mountains of Tupperware? Ready to reuse, recycle, repurpose, or donate? Tossing should be a last resort. Translation: let's find another use for things, including hurricane water. Water plants, fill the pet water bowls, wash produce, or wash the smelly dogs. A fresher smelling house will be your reward.

# Stuff and Beyond

## What's in Your Drawers?

"I found five nail clippers and stabbed my thumb twice with the same pushpin while searching for a paperclip in your top desk drawer. I took the coins for pain and suffering."

These are the words my husband texted while I vacationed by a lake. He included a photo of the offending drawer's contents and one of his punctured thumb. I'm surprised he didn't mention the over-stretched, hazardous rubber band around my pens, pencils and highlighters, a multi-color array of writing implements. He could have gotten severely wounded.

What could I text back except, "I love my office supplies. About that $2.08 in change? Don't spend it all in one place."

Once I arrived home and settled into my desk to write, I pulled hard on the top drawer to find an assortment of useful items the hubby didn't mention. Nail files, sticky notes, tiny notepads, and my grandfather's one-hole punch. I saw large clamps and clips, my old auto-inking address stamp, and a pack of Stim-U-Dent plaque removers. The plaque removers are little more than thin slivers of wood, basically fancy toothpicks introduced to me by my father-in-law.

The best find was fourteen dollars squirreled away for pizza delivery tips and other such vital emergencies. The hubby swiped my change but left the bills. Guess he didn't have all that much pain and suffering.

Everybody needs a junk drawer. But when people plunder through your messy drawers, it's natural to feel shame about your treasures. What's in your drawers? OK, people, minds out of the gutters. Let's try to keep all this disorganization chatter G-Rated.

## One Man's Trash

My home office with the big picture window I love so much looks like it ate a pine tree and threw up paper. There must be treasure under all those papers, or at least bills I need to find and pay right away. No time for sentimentality with potential late fees under the minutiae. Or is there? A little de-cluttering is a good thing—it's not like I'm procrastinating from doing the dusting. Going through drawers counts as a worthwhile chore.

In a desk drawer and in desktop organizers, I found old To-Do Lists a-plenty. Each one included the same sentiment: *simplify, de-clutter, purge, find missing* \_\_fill in the blank. Also, *use gift cards* and *write* were included on many lists.

In addition to the lists I found my real treasures. Small slips of paper with fun moments to remember like: Joe's first shave; a tiny plastic bag holding Sam's two teeth pulled for braces; and Sarah's love note saying, "All I want for Christmas is a boxer puppy from Fort Mill like I saw in the paper."

Being a compulsive record keeper, I'd made a list

of funny quotes by the kids. Finding this gem made my day. Here are a few quotes:

"Acne and Bradycardia is what Sam used to have," said ten-year-old Sarah about her brother. It was actually called Apnea, not Acne. Sam replied, "I didn't have Acne and Bradycardia, it was Jr. Acne."

During *the talk* with ten-year-old Joe, I was drawing a woman's fallopian tubes on a white board when Joe said, "Where's that thing Daddy had to cut? You remember—the Biblical Cord."

I came across a funny conversation I'd written down when ten-year-old Joe and Sam were discussing possible Halloween costumes. Please pardon the potty-room talk.

I told them, "You can come up with compound words and each dress like one of those words. Then you walk together as one costume. Your sister Danielle and her friend Kelsey were a compound word one year. One wore a giant aluminum foil-covered cardboard star and the other wore a reindeer hat and stuck play money all over her shirt. Get it? They were *Starbucks*."

"Oh, I get it," they said in unison. The boys came up with "grapevine," "fire truck," and a dozen other compound words. Finally, Joe said, "I know. I can be 'Go' and Sam can be 'Nad.'"

I was still snickering at the memory of Joe's comment when I spotted a brand-new note from sixteen-year-old Sarah that was stuck to the computer. Her lovely round letters announced: "All I want for Christmas is a cheap but safe and good-enough-truck and here's why: If you don't have to drive the boys and me around, you can spend more time organizing and writing for that class you love so much. I can buy groceries and bring you Starbucks so you can keep on writing. Then you won't have to rush to write late the night before your class. You can do what you tell us, 'Get your work done ahead of time so you won't feel stressed.'"

That little four-door truck has lots of miles on it now, six years later. What's in drawer number two? Decluttering is way more fun than housecleaning and bill paying. I wonder what's in those office cabinets. The bills can wait till tomorrow.

## Consignment Worthy?

What's a person to do with the unworn clothes smothering the air right out of the closet? It's a common dilemma, especially if a person is an impulsive sale shopper. I don't like to shop but man oh man, I sure can get sucked in by a well-placed sale sign and bring home multiples of a dreadful yet super comfortable shirt in several colors. Why? Because then my shopping is done. Or at least I think so until I realize how ridiculous the shirts look on me several times a week.

Tossing them is out of the question, as landfills are always a last resort for me. If it can be handed down, sold, donated, or refurbished into a T-shirt quilt by my daughter, I'm all for it. Clear that closet. But I refuse to thoughtlessly toss usable items into the trash.

In need of more closet space, I recruited that same daughter to help me weed out some unnecessary apparel. She was firm but kind. Together we eliminated dozens of items from my overstuffed closet. Even after purging, the racks and shelves looked plenty full. But at least my clothes were less smashed together like paper in a printer.

As I tried on every single piece of clothing, my

daughter rehung or folded the clothes and separated them into bins for donation or consignment. I'm ashamed to admit several tops had tags still adorning their sleeves so I decided to try consigning for a change. Loading three laundry baskets and lugging them to the van, I envisioned making a few bucks so off I went to sell my assets.

The first consignment store's young clerks took my baskets with what looked like genuine grins, suggesting I might look around the store while waiting for their decision. Perusing the store, I noticed a, let's just say, most unattractive green leatherette vest that was cracked around all the seams. *My stuff is so much better than this. Oh yeah. I might leave with enough money for a nice family dinner at Chili's.*

My phone buzzed with a text from the girl across the room. "Inspection complete." I went to the desk expecting to retrieve my mostly empty laundry baskets and a "nice little piece of money," as my mother would say.

Instead, I heard, "Thanks so much for coming in. Unfortunately, we have plenty of these types of clothes, but please continue shopping and come back again. You might also try the consignment place across the parking lot."

I stumbled out the door hauling the rejected wardrobe to my car and drove across the parking lot to consignment store number two. I'll admit my clothes are not expensive name brands. Why should they be since I can get great deals from Kohl's at thirty percent off of another thirty percent off? But I'm a little offended that the teenage clerks deemed my fine clothes not consignment-worthy. Even those items with store tags still hanging on their sleeves. They must only know about teenage clothes in size double zero and such.

Leaving my loot in the car, I went into the other place. The well-groomed gentleman there said, "We only look at clothes less than two years old, on hangers, and they cannot be from Gap, Old Navy, Kohl's, or Banana Republic."

I thanked him and headed for my van. Choosing to ignore the hanger rule, I retrieved a couple of neatly folded Talbot's and J Jill tops and took them back into the store to see if they were acceptable.

"The Talbot's lettering must be black, not red or white, and everything must be on hangers. But it looks like a couple of your things might do," the man said.

I thanked him again, strolled back to my hot car, and drove my three full baskets home. He didn't need my couple of things. Consignment rules galore meant all items bought over two years ago were pretty much worthless.

After researching many options, I chose a well-organized thrift store that hires young adults with special needs and provides them with vocational rehab and job coaching. After donating my clothes, I even did a little shopping there and checked out with a smiling young man who was learning to wrap and bag.

Lisa Batten Kunkleman

Who needs consignment? Not me. Never again for this girl. I'm back to donating. It's a better fit.

## Mysterious Recycling Phenomenon

I don't know why, but the day after our mini blizzard, which in North Carolina can mean an inch or two of snow and ice, there was a roll out garbage and recycling bin phenomenon. It was the first day of clear roads after our little *snow-event-extended-weekend*, when on my morning walk, I noticed all the trash cans and recycling bins were chock-full and overflowing. Almost like the week after Christmas. The recycling bins were especially bulging. Cardboard and crushed-up boxes crammed and stacked so high, the lids were left dangling to the back, unable to close.

I looked for a pattern as I passed our neighbors' houses and wondered what people do on snow days to accumulate so much cardboard and recyclables? Do they clean out the garage? Do they clean out their attic? Drawers and closets? Or do they finally get around to opening those Christmas gifts they don't actually need or want?

Like my shiny red mixer, still inside the untouched FedEx box. I'll need it when I need it but since I haven't yet, it remains box-bound. One of the neighbors' smashed boxes once housed a waffle-stick maker.

Another contained a holey meatloaf pan with a grease-snatcher trap underneath. Wonder what's deeper in the bin? Boxes from a snow cone maker, a cotton candy machine, an electric cheese grater, maybe?

Curious, but not curious enough to dig through people's bins, I spied long rolls of decent-looking wrapping paper sticking out the top of one, and a fat roll of snowflake decorated duct tape on the curb below. I have to admit the thought crossed my mind to snag those items if I walked by there again. Another can was filled with large chunks of foam like what's inside a cushion. Interesting. Wonder if the dog ate it.

By the time I decided to adjust my walking route to pick up the duct tape that still lay in the gutter for two more days, it was gone. Darn. Maybe I'll see something fun after the next snow days.

I should consider cleaning out a few of my own closets and drawers during the next snow days. Nah, I'll keep relaxing by the fire with soup and coffee, taking snowy hikes with the family, and letting the clutter build up. But not thick layers of accumulation. Only a little layer, a thin dusting, like our North Carolina snow.

# Life, The Great Classroom

## Rest in Peace

    A peaceful morning turned tragic with my one shove of the outside playhouse to the far side of the patio. Sam said, "Look at this, guys!" Suddenly all three of our four-year-olds said, "Ooo yuck. What is that thing?" Upon close inspection I saw a little webbed foot protruding from the ooo yuck. A poor little toad was a casualty of my constant shifting of toys, bikes, playhouses, and various and sundry items strewn everywhere. I'd been praying that I'd learn to ignore all this clutter, knowing one day I'd miss the assortment that decorates our yard and home so colorfully, making us look like we run a preschool. But that's another story. Back to our tragedy.

    After I tossed the toad to the far side of the grass, Sam screamed as if he'd just stepped on a snake tail. "No, I want to show Dad!" Feeling like a big meanie for not thinking before tossing, I walked with Sam to retrieve the squishy little guy. He wanted to hold the toad in his bare hand and wasn't at all grossed out by the icky sensation he must have felt. Like good students in line behind our leader, Sam, we were led through the back door, marched down the long hall, and guided up the stairs to Dad's office to show him the ooo yuck resting in the palm of the now satisfied, future Dr. Sam. Once Dad said, "Oh, you have a dead toad," or something equally thrilling for Sam and his siblings, we marched back downstairs and out the kitchen door to perform a toad funeral. After we decided frog legs were edible and therefore were technically food scraps, we solemnly walked to the compost pile and found a good rut in the red clay among the eggshells and banana peels. Sam gently laid the toad mush in just the right spot in the dry red dirt.

We proceeded with the funeral as each child respectfully placed a little scoop of dirt on top of the dearly departed. We each said a word of prayer and a few more words about what a nice little toad he must have been. We prayed that his parents or family and friends wouldn't be too sad when they realized Toad was gone. We even reassured ourselves that maybe Toad was already deathly ill and that we helped him die quickly and with no pain. I had my doubts about how painless a death by playhouse squishing would have been, but I kept those thoughts all to myself.

We sang "Jesus Loves Me" for our closing hymn. Finally, the firstborn of my triplets, Joe, took a piece of broken shingle he'd found on the ground and placed it on the dirt. He then gently patted the shingle's worn surface. We quietly headed back to the house to mourn in our own personal ways. Realizing that Joe wasn't with us, I turned to see his last contribution to the funeral proceedings. As a final act of respect for our fallen friend Toad, Joe, who believes in doing things in proper military manner, gave a one-gun salute by pulling down his pants and watering the gravesite. Hopefully this act of reverence gave Toad an appropriate send off to Amphibian Heaven. Rest in peace, little guy.

## Walnuts and My Tom Sawyer Moment

My twenty-year-old son Sam walks barefoot in our backyard picking up walnuts with his long, thin, size-thirteen toes. It's a special talent I passed down to him with my own sizable hoof.

When the nuts fall off the black walnut tree, the nearly baseball-sized hard green outer shell is a threat to an uncovered head. As the green shell dries to black and falls off the actual nut deep inside, the black shells become a nasty nuisance. It takes gloves and rakes to remove the staining shells. It's much smarter to remove them in the early hard stage instead of waiting till they dye your hands and shoes black.

A light bulb flickers in my head. I'm not Mark Twain and this is not really Tom Sawyer tricking folks into whitewashing his fence, but I can't help thinking this seems like a good way to get the walnuts picked out of the yard.

I say to Sam, "Think you could hit that sweet gum tree with a walnut?"

"Which one?" he asks.

"That big one in that leafy natural area. The squirrels haul the nuts over there to chomp into the hard shells anyway. Never let a squirrel bite you. They must have teeth of steel."

"Mama, I got bad aim," Sam says after pitching the first nut to the right of the tree.

"Yeah and you also 'got' bad grammar," I tell my six-foot-three baby boy who actually has impeccable grammar.

"Naw, my grammar's all right."

He throws one walnut after the other, hitting the tree and splattering the green outer shell about every third throw.

Next thing I know, here comes his daddy, saying, "Want me to show you how to hit that tree?"

This is working out even better than I expected. His father is not a bystander.

"There we go," says Daddy Dan when he hits the tree. And I hear, "All right! Did you see that one, Sam? Did you see that nut explode when it hit the tree? Maybe that sweet gum tree will feel the pain and stop dropping spikey sweet gum balls."

"Hey! I want to play," says our oldest daughter, flouncing down the deck steps to join the competition. Perfect. *Many hands make light work*, as they say. And

## Just Because I Used To Could

like Tom Sawyer's friends, my family never even knows they've been snookered into completing a job. Well done.

## Squabble, Tiff, or Spat: Just Fix It

It's amazing how a small disagreement can turn into a large, loud, ridiculous argument in a flippin' fuchsia minute. (That's a play on red-hot minute.) Mere seconds before, life is coasting along fine and suddenly, one person's mouth opens and says something without knowing it will be taken the wrong way by the other party and BAM! The peace is split wide open. Torn and ripped with a zillion jagged edges, and it all started because one person is either insensitive or the other is overly sensitive or perhaps it's both. And a spat is born.

Maybe it doesn't even matter what was said or who was testy or touchy. What matters is where this event takes those squabbling people. It matters if the relationship is an unhealthy one, where the event may dissolve the relationship. Sometimes, that is for the best. But for people who really care about maintaining their relationship, there are several options. Through years of co-existing with my own family, I've observed and utilized some of the following ways of dealing with day-to-day tiffs. Use these options with care, as they are often not the best ways to solve issues. Sometimes these methods backfire, making the whole mess even messier.

## Just Because I Used To Could

Pouting is always a possibility. Quiet and ugly-faced on some people, this is often effective if kept up long enough to push the other party to give if he or she cannot stand to go without reciprocated conversation. It may have the opposite effect if one party really enjoys the silent treatment. An introvert may never give in to a pouter and may relish the silence for an indefinite period.

Stomping around and slamming things like cabinet doors is another option. Be careful not to hurt pets or other people in all the dramatics. Muttering or even expounding to oneself about how aggravating and unfair the other party is can sometimes be effective if one party tends to feel guilty about things and the slammer-talker is good at making people feel guilt. Southern women tend to be masters of this technique.

Pretending like nothing happened and coming back to the other party with normal conversation, food, gifts, and/or even a gentle shoulder massage is an option that works quite nicely for some couples who argue on purpose just to get this response. This is especially effective for tactically sensitive people and those who get their way by kissing up.

It doesn't really matter who was wrong or right, although we can argue that point in circles forever and never get an answer. What matters is that if you care for a person, just fix it. I'd like to say let it go but I shouldn't due to a recent blockbuster movie and song making people a bit tired of that phrase. But that's what needs to happen. Really. We don't have enough time to hold grudges with people we love. Lighten up. If you can't laugh it off, you might try praying for hearts to be softened so forgiveness can occur. What have you got to lose? Here, in case you've never prayed or don't believe in prayer, I'll start one for you. "Dear Father, please help us to lighten up, enjoy life and love each other..." Now how hard was that?

## And Evil is Her Name

My husband used to call me Sweet Thing. I hated it because he only did it when I was being anything but sweet. Today, he texted me asking, "What evil are you up to?" He switched from Sweet Thing to Evil thinking it would bug me. I actually liked it.

I said, "I'd rather you call me Evil or even Sweevil than call me Sweet Thing when we all know it's not true."

I wondered what he thought I did all day. My main job has always been to try to make sure everybody was happy or at least not an emotional, stressed-out wreck. My stars, we had a twenty-four-year-old, engaged daughter who worked three jobs and was also a student. Add to that our seventeen-year-old triplets with enough schoolwork daily to fill a week, plus their extracurriculars. The Kunkleman pots stayed full to the top. If even one emotional pot blew, the household was in big trouble. I did what I could to keep everybody's pot at a simmer or at best a slow boil.

My husband needed an example of why I wasn't always such a sweet thing. I told him this: Elder Daughter called to see if I could help her shop for wedding reception supplies. Younger Daughter requested we have a family dinner because as she said, "Everybody else's family is able to sit down together and eat a home-cooked meal every night so why can't we?" *Yeah, right. Sure they do. Just like everybody's family is neat and clean in Facebook photos and perfectly stellar in Christmas letters.*

I know I'm not supposed to admit this in my quest for Mother of the Year but here's a shocker. I had a life too. I told Elder Daughter I had an assignment due for my writing class, to which she graciously said, "It's OK, we can shop another day." She learned that guilt trick from me. Of course, I felt like Motherzilla of the Bride and was about to call her back to say I'd meet her, but Younger Daughter texted, "What's the dinner plan?" It's hard to read emotion in a text but I knew she had her eyebrows raised in a pleading position. I texted back, "BBQ chicken."

I threw some BBQ sauce on chicken tenders, which by some miracle were actually in our fridge, and requested that one of our very capable two sons slide them into the oven while I ran errands with Elder Daughter. Then a text came in asking if I could help Younger Daughter with her US History tonight because she was in dire need and had a test the next day. I, of course, texted back saying, "Yes." Then I remembered I promised Younger Son I would help edit an English paper and try to find research material online with him. So, as you can see, I did nothing all day but eat Peanut M&M's and binge watch *Friends* for a tenth go-round.

## Just Because I Used To Could

Here's where Evil entered. Well, not exactly prize-winning evil, but maybe I could get an honorable mention. I had a deep, dark secret. I watched *The Bachelor*. It was the final rose night, and I was needed everywhere except in front of the TV. My decadent side wished I could shirk all that helpfulness and watch the show with Elder Son, who had no homework for a change. We could pick a suitable fiancée for that poor bachelor. Yep. It was shallow entertainment with way too much smooching, but Elder Son and I looked forward to this idiocy every week along with all the other viewers who had kept the show going for twelve seasons. We are different from those people, however, because we only watched for the exotic locations. Younger Daughter enjoyed the show even more than her brother, but she had work to do, which was another reason I felt guilty for wanting to watch the show without her. Dang it. My mama gave me an overload of the guilt gene.

After shopping, eating supper together, and getting schoolwork underway, at last it was 10 p.m. My husband, a delightful man, but not as guilt-ridden over his children's schoolwork as I, expected our Monday night date time to watch our favorite detective show, *Castle*. I would have loved that under normal circumstances. But for tonight I preferred to watch my recorded version of *The Bachelor* where the star would give out that final rose. I wanted to see the final episode with my own eyes, not hear all about it on-line and on *Good Morning America* the next day. Which girl would he send home in tears? Was that too much to ask? Was I really Evil to want that shallow time just for me? I mean us. My tall, muscular, Elder Son who always fell asleep before the end and woke up wanting to know who went home, and me? I was thinking of my husband's own good anyway. He looked tired so he probably needed to get to sleep early. We could watch *Castle* together tomorrow night, when he was more rested.

## Auditing Life

    I've always wanted to be a professional student. If time and money allowed, I'd be signing up to audit all kinds of classes. No tests or projects for grades, thank you. Now that we have an empty nest, how fun it would be to sneak into the back of my three college-kids' classes and learn from their teachers. Then my kids and I could converse about all the knowledge we're absorbing.
    Speaking of absorbing, I want to learn about moss, for example. I understand that good old absorbent moss can help scientists monitor environmental pollution levels. If the moss disappears, look out, earthlings. The same thing happens with birds falling from above and

bee populations dwindling. There are also far too many tales of five-legged frog sightings online these days. That can't be a good sign for life, as we know it.

I'd probably enjoy classes like *The Joy of Garbage, The History of Toys,* and *Kitchen Chemistry* but not so much *Underwater Basket Weaving* and *Advanced Calculus*. I'd rather learn survival skills just in case I'm ever plopped in the wilderness and have to find my way home without starving or worse, becoming somebody's lunch.

Learning about *parenting* before I had four kids to practice on would have made sense. Hmmm. I just realized people practice medicine, practice law and they're supposed to already know what they're doing. So maybe practicing parenting isn't so bad. Our kids all turned out pretty darn good to be products of a couple of practitioners.

I'd also like a redo lesson on child development and abnormal psychology, which is either a funny or pathetic desire since I'm a psychology major. While I was in grad school to become a guidance counselor, one wise professor said, "Take all that you learn in school and either toss it away or tuck it in your back pocket if you feel the need. You're going to be winging it through work and life with whatever you absorb and decide is worth using." And that's why he was teaching counselors how to counsel.

It would have been lots more fun to audit those psych classes instead of cramming like crazy for exams and retaining a pittance of that material. My professor was right. No parent ever asked me, "What psychological theorist's method do you use in your practice?" Ha. I was *practicing* psychology and counseling for all those years. In an ah-ha moment, I realize I've spent my whole life practicing pretty much everything. Maybe the whole world is filled with practitioners. Are there really any experts? I'm not so sure.

Don't most of us wonder how things are made? I should binge watch YouTube *How To's.* How in the world is duct tape made without getting all stuck together? Why doesn't super glue stick to the bottle? And what about the infinite supply of unanswerable questions? Has anyone besides me wondered if sea level would change if you took every animal and boat out of the water at the same time? My mind is a whorl of questions. Why doesn't my whole body get wrinkled in the water? It's only my fingers and toes. Did you ever wonder about that? So many questions and so few answers.

I'd love to take a field trip to see icebergs and another trip to lie in a hammock in a rain forest to watch for iguanas and toucans while listening for howler monkeys and bare-throated bellbirds. I have no idea what the last two are, but I heard from a rain-forest ranger in Puerto Rico that they're pretty amazing.

I want to conquer those infernal fears that keep me nestled in my comfort zone, afraid to explore new heights and depths. Well, maybe not that since I'm afraid of heights and am claustrophobic in submarines. I do like caves though, which is kinda contradictory to the whole fear of tight places. Oops. I digressed. That stifling fear whispers, *don't do it*, because of age, aches and pains, or crash landing after falling from something really high up.

If I'm honest, much of the time I hold back because I am afraid of being judged as selfishly wasting time doing frivolous things. I'd like to be that person who couldn't give two hoots what other people think. That free-spirited, eccentric character every family needs who relishes life and provides spice to any conversation. If that's my plan, I'd better get on with it since middle age is turning out to be a little fickle on the knees, eyes, and well, the rest of the body. I'm ready to hobble on out there while I can, to explore and learn in this incredible classroom called "Life."

## My Ancestors Keep Me Up At Night

My ancestors keep me up at night. Not in a haunting, spooky, hover-above-the-bed way but in an addictive, I can't seem to drag myself away from Ancestry.com kind-of-way. My obsession with family history intensifies with each passing year. I'm afraid other people will take precious knowledge to their graves like my grandparents did, leaving more unanswerable questions. The problem is, it's hard to know what the questions are until there's a mystery to solve and then it is too late because oftentimes, there is no one left who can help provide answers.

Oh, how I wish I had my dad here to fill in some blanks for me in the family tree and make this research much easier. I almost waited too late to become curious about family history, but thank goodness Daddy and I talked frequently about historical topics while spending time together working jigsaw puzzles or taking walks.

I thought I had control of this addiction, but I don't. I plan to blog or write for class but when I sit at the computer, those old relatives get into my head. "Check your messages," they say. "You might have a new DNA cousin." Or "You might have a hint about your Viking relatives, that gory branch of the tree that intrigues your sons."

Sometimes I think I'll unwind before going to bed, so I sit at my desk for a minute. Yeah right. I check my e-mail one last time and make the mistake of clicking on the one from Ancestry.com that says, "Possible Record Matches in Batten, Kunkleman Family Tree." That minute turns into several hours. Next thing I know it's two in the morning, and I'm so wired up from all the juicy news stories and black sheep, there's no way I can get to sleep.

So, I print the stories and punch holes in the pages. Into my binders they go. I should probably worry about the grind of the printer and the click of the notebook disturbing my snoring husband on the other side of my office door, but I can't pull myself away from the latest clue leading to answers about mysterious missing links. Like a chocoholic who can't stop till the family size bag of M&Ms is flat and empty, I can't stop checking for new DNA matches or adding one new name to one of my five family trees. Every time I add something new, a little green leaf pops up telling me I have two, four, or even ten hints to check from that tiny morsel of information.

    I feel my pulse race and my eyes widen, hoping that a missing piece to my massive tree will finally turn up. Like an impossible five-thousand-piece puzzle with no picture to guide me, I lust to connect the pieces. It's like an obsession. Daddy, a former jigsaw enthusiast, now among our ancestors, would understand. I can see him now, stooped over the round table on the sun porch working a puzzle saying, "Just one more piece. Then I'll stop. Just one more piece." Now it's me, saying to myself, "Just one more person. Then I'll stop. Just one more."

## Beeps, and Bongs, and Chimes, Oh My!

These days, I can get nagged from every corner of the house even when I'm all alone except for the animals. I'm used to my family ever so gently telling me when I'm doing something wrong or forgetting things, but lately I'm getting reminders from my electronics, too. It's becoming a bit much.

I need to set my phone's inbox so it doesn't ping and ting every time I get a ding dang e-mail! I will check it myself when I get good and ready, thank you very much.

I hear beeps and bongs and chimes no matter where I go. I can't figure out which appliance is telling me what to do when.

This morning, as I loaded the dishwasher, I heard an unfamiliar delicate ping from across the room. I asked the dogs, "Do you hear that?" They looked around the kitchen, and seeing no movement, were obviously confused too.

After hearing the sound repeat itself three times, I walked to the table and checked my new phone, and there it was. My husband had sent a text that needed immediate attention. Of course it did. That pretty sound came from my brand-new phone with all kinds of new noises that I don't recognize. I knew this because it dinged all night announcing mail from *Reader's Digest*, the local performing arts center box office, and Restaurant.com, since those couldn't wait till daylight. I guess I'd been subconsciously conditioned to ignore any dang ding. I planned to adjust the sounds later, but I rebelled, not wanting to be ordered around by a bossy piece of metal the size of a pork chop. Take that. OK, fine. I'll silence it but not because it demanded I obey.

If I leave the laundry in the dryer ten minutes longer than I should, I get a reminder song of "do do do do." It's much prettier than it looks on paper. If I stand and look in the fridge with even a few seconds of indecision, the darn thing sings me a melody that says, "You're letting the cold air out so close the door, woman." I sing back, "You're lucky you're so full of condiments, there's no room left for old moldy food. So just hush."

I kinda like the sounds of the dishwasher. Its pretty voice sings to let me know it's done. No demands or judgment. I can leave it as long as I want, and the mugs and plates won't wrinkle or sour. Finally, I have time to check my phone. Now where did I put it? The electrician is supposed to call before he comes to fix our motion lights. Oh shoot! A fine time to put my phone on silent. Where's that ding dang phone when I need it?

## Tim Tation

I lost far too many hours of my life today. Hours I will never get back. With the house to myself, instead of writing, which is a writer's job, I decided to act like I did in college after each major test and reward myself by doing nothing. Nothing constructive, that is. I used to lounge around in my apartment on the brown plaid sofa or orange shag carpet and watch MTV music videos for hours at a time. Starting in 1981, MTV was the newest TV phenomenon. Some of my first video binge watching included REO Speedwagon's "Keep on Loving You," Phil Collins's "In the Air Tonight," and Stevie Nicks's "Stop Draggin' My Heart Around." Man, that was good music.

Today, in this technological age, with plenty of DVR'd shows and Netflix available at a moment's notice, I choose to watch my favorite show, *This Is Us*. Not only do I watch a couple of episodes, I stay up until 2 a.m. watching all of them. Since I am behind on episodes and don't want to hear a spoiler about what's going to happen, it's actually kind of important that I catch up. How's that for rationalizing my laziness?

Here's an analogy, which exhibits a bit more of my expert rationalization skills. Goodness gracious! It is not even 8 a.m. and I literally just took a fork to what was left of a multi-layer chocolate cake. Didn't even bother with a plate. Just stood there eating it while I refilled my coffee. It seemed better to eat it and get it out of sight than leave it around, distracting me all day. It was just best to hush up that nasty troublemaker, Tim Tation!!!!

That's what I do with this TV series. I totally give in to Tim Tation. I attempt to ignore other voices like Shoulda Ben, but with little luck. Shoulda Ben stands on my shoulder nagging about phone calls I should make to old friends and distant relatives. And what about the homebound people that my church tends to? They could probably use a card or a casserole. Tim Tation says that can wait till tomorrow because I need to catch up on *This is Us*. I agree. Laziness 1; Productiveness 0.

I try to return to watching my third episode to finish up Season One on Netflix, but again, a voice interrupts me. Shoulda Ben destroys my solitude, ranting at me about writing thank you notes, and that drawer-full of Thinking of You cards I could be sending out.

Shoulda Ben starts grumbling at me about cleaning those disgusting corners and baseboards that I would be ashamed even for a cleaning person to see. Y'all know what I mean. I am not the first person who would clean the house before allowing somebody to come clean it for pay.

And here I sit. Wisha Could is sitting here with me, tossing out ideas I wish I could write about, but I can't decide where to start. Wisha Could says I should turn off the TV and do some writing already. The DVR won't erase the shows. Worry later about Shoulda Ben, and spend some time with Ithinka Might for inspiration. As if hours spent watching an incredible show that makes me laugh, cry, and binge watch isn't inspiration enough. I'm actually absorbing cleverness with each episode. Should I get up and do something more constructive? Maybe later. Tim Tation is sitting here waiting to watch Season Two with me.

# Empty Nesting

## Controlling What is Easy

Is this a midlife crisis? Am I making conscious choices to act in certain ways? This is the morning after we gave our three high school seniors a birthday dinner, and I'm preparing myself for that stinking empty nest syndrome. I'm afraid to enter my office piled-high with kids' files, baby books, and pictures because I might get the urge to reminisce.

Resisting the urge to go into the office to write, I choose instead to become Suzy Homemaker because someone just might drop by and see my disaster of a kitchen. I decide not to procrastinate on cleaning for a change, deciding that it's better to procrastinate on writing because nobody can run a finger through the dust in my head. Well, nobody except the writing class I go to tomorrow and admit that I have nothing worth a darn to read to my critique group thanks to my sudden urge to clean.

I decide to do the dishes by hand. Yep. By hand. First, I empty the still full dishwasher from the night before and put away all those dishes. Then I wash all the dishes that wouldn't fit in the last load of the evening, and I do them by hand with an empty dishwasher staring at me asking, "What in the heck are you doing? I'm sitting here with my door open waiting for you to fill me up and push my buttons, and you're elbow-deep in suds and dishes. Are you nuts?"

Maybe. Maybe not. The warm, sudsy water embraces my hands, reminding me of how I'd run perfect-temperature water in each of our four kids' baths when they were little. They went from dirty to clean and oh-so-snuggly. We'd wrap them in kid towels that had a corner folded over for the head so they could wear them like capes.

They'd run around and giggle, flapping their towels like flying squirrels before being tucked into bed for stories and answering our question, "What was the best part of your day?" I wrote their answers in journals to peruse with them someday, decades later. Who knew decades pass so quickly?

I decide I need a little time to transform something from dirty to clean and wet to dry. I go from a counter full of crumbs and greasy cookware to a counter full of nothing unless I want it to be there. I have complete control over things I can pick up and put down exactly where I want them, like I used to be able to do with my kids. I end up with a kitchen looking neat and in order. Me. I did it. Not the dishwasher. Controlling my feelings about the empty nest is difficult, so I'm controlling what is easy.

## Miracle of the Condiments

You may remember the Bible story, the miracle of the loaves and fishes multiplying to feed the masses. A couple of birds have flown back into our empty nest for the summer. That means I need more room in my refrigerator for fresh vegetables to feed the coeds. They've eaten cafeteria buffet and junk food the entire school year, and it's my job to boost their immune systems while the produce stands are loaded with fresh crops.

I'm proud to say I'm now known as a master salad maker and veggie smoothie queen-mother. These lucky kids are living in a health-food paradise. That is, with all the fruits and veggies that I can squeeze in the fridge. They won't last long on the kitchen counter.

So here I am doing the dreaded fridge clean out, chucking lots of unnecessary, unhealthy, and expired condiments to make some room for the healthy stuff. My large sink becomes a holding spot for discards, full of outdated bottles and jars of condiments and beet remains. I had to force myself to get physical with all that gross gunk in the containers, rinse them out, and properly dispose of them in the recycle bin. I'm ashamed to admit three jars were too much for me to scrape clean so they went in the trash. Guilt may haunt me enough that I go digging through the outside trash bin to retrieve them and try harder to protect the good old environment.

I survey the situation. And dang! It hardly looks any different from when I started except it's missing a few sticky spots. How is it possible to clean out my fridge, and still end up with a fridge that is chock-full?

I've contemplated this dilemma and decided using a cooler on the counter won't do as a permanent kitchen decoration. I may dive back into the fridge and search for more expiration dates from four years ago like the Worcestershire sauce I poured down the big sink drain. I figure it must have turned to Drano by now and could possibly eat up some cloggy plaque. I'll tackle the fridge clearing again because my counter is full of actual food in need of some cold air. Man cannot live by condiments alone.

## And Then There Were None

My husband Dan and I spent many a day strolling our triplet babies through the mall in their extra-long, stadium-seat triple stroller. Our older daughter, Danielle, even at the age of seven, was like their third parent and had lots of practice being the spokesperson for her babies. After all, she was the one who insisted she needed a sibling. Every few yards, people said, "You really have your hands full," or, "Better you than me."

She didn't even notice some of the negative or totally inappropriate comments people made like how they would end it all if they were in our shoes, or personal questions asking for details of how in the world we got three babies. I had no intention of teaching these folks the birds and the bees in front of our seven-year-old.

Danielle stood up straight and expounded on how great it was having a house filled with babies. About how we had three laps which was just the right number to hold all the babies.

When Danielle left for college a mere eleven years later, her neat and hollow room was an empty chasm I avoided. I hated walking by her door, so I went the long way around through our bedroom to get to the other kids' rooms. It was a tough transition for the five of us left at home. Their third parent had moved away.

Four years later, the triplets, as tweens, filled that void by stealing Danielle's room and booting her to the guest room, deciding she wouldn't be a full-time resident again. Sarah had her own room and bathroom to herself. The boys had separate rooms for the first time ever and shared a bathroom formerly fought over by the girls. Helpful hint: If you can avoid having sisters share a bathroom, life is probably easier especially in the morning.

We never would have believed eighteen years could zip by in a hot minute when we were hip deep in diapers, but it did. What a carnival it's been for a quarter of a century with our four kids and their friends everywhere we looked, running through the yard and the house and climbing trees like monkeys. At times life at our house looked like a circus crossed with a county fair and at others, like a prep school study center crossed with a music and dance studio. Fast forward through ballgames, choral and band concerts, marching band competitions, dance recitals, church youth group trips and mission work and the time just flew. To borrow a phrase from one of our favorite movies, *The Princess Bride*, "It's inconceivable."

Nearing graduation day, friends said, "How're you doing?" and "I'm praying for you," and "It's going to be so quiet at your house with a triple empty nest." It's a wonder I didn't run out of tears before the big day. I didn't. I cried plenty. Tears of pride and joy and of pondering what lay ahead.

August came and everything changed. We'd go to the kitchen and there were no crumbs on the counter or bowls in the sink. No heads to rub or bodies to hug. Nobody said, "Hey, Mom, can you call these vocab words out to me while I finish making my lunch?" Nobody said, "Hey, Mom, can you sign this form? I got a letter grade off for not bringing it in yesterday." Nobody said, "Hey, Mom, if you're making an egg, can you make me one too?" Right before they left, as independence was setting in, this often switched to, "Hey, Mom, I'm making eggs. You want me to make you some?"

Oh, man. I'd look down, sometimes even tearing up and reply, "Absolutely. Thank you so much. Looks like you're ready to fly outa this nest since you can make your own eggs."

With the last goodbye hugs, Dan and I were a

couple again, alone with the animals, wandering around this big old house and farm. There's that saying about silence being deafening. I finally got it.

When the kids first left, friends again shared their kind words. They texted of their thoughts and prayers for us as they knew how big this instant triple change would be. Their prayers must have been answered because I expected to be out of Kleenex and mopping my flood of tears with paper towels by now while scaring the animals with my incessant wailing. Instead, I was less weepy than I was in the awful pre-departure period when my eyes puddled at the very mention of the kids leaving.

Even though not living in our house, Danielle and her husband, Ben, felt the sudden mass departure. They too felt the silence and did their best to add some noise and keep up the clatter and laughter having their friends play cards and games and eat food galore at our house. Lucky for us they settled nearby and hung out at the farm with us often, which was more valuable to us than they will ever know.

The animals took it pretty hard at first and stayed with us in every room of the house needing consolation and a lap to make furry. So at least we still felt needed. They had a look that said, "Are you two really all we get now?" The dogs wanted to go in and out of the front door every few minutes just to see if anything had changed. I knew the feeling.

## Snow Day Monopoly

Having our boys home from college during a few rare snow days was such a treat. We cooked, ate, watched suspenseful TV by the fire, and hiked through the fields and woods. It sure beat using the extra time at home to work on my to-do list. I also had help tending our menagerie of critters, and the critters had additional laps and hands besides mine.

But now the nest is empty once again. My brother made fun of me asking, "So how's that empty nest going? Is it ever empty?"

I'm loving that I see the kids one, two, three, or even all four at the same time, and more often than I expected when they left for college. I know it can change in an instant, so living in the moment and enjoying whoever comes and goes is working out well. I'm just thankful that they love home and want to come check in now and then.

We played Monopoly on one of the snow days. Our oldest daughter, Danielle, and her husband, Ben, ventured out on the icy roads and found the path to our house not too treacherous. Deciding to go through the game closet for something we hadn't played in a long time, Ben suggested Monopoly. I have bad memories of the first and last time we played this with our kids. Three out of our four kids were in elementary school and within the first fifteen minutes of the game, my husband, Dan, had already sent seven-year-old Joe into bankruptcy. I suggested we give him a break and help him out of his first-ever financial bind, but Dan said we should follow the rules and teach them how it all works. Needless to say, the game didn't continue much longer and ended with sad bankruptcies and disagreeing parents.

This time would be different. After all, they were college students. We started out fine except for Sam, who either landed on *Pay Taxes* or *Just Visiting Jail* or *Chance* sending him to jail without passing *Go* or collecting two hundred dollars. My mother instinct kicked in thinking this would be round two of early bankruptcy for yet another son. I was preparing to deal with him to help him out when his luck changed. Before I could blink, the man-child owned hotels and I was going broke, never getting a set of the same color properties, never even getting a house.

## Lisa Batten Kunkleman

After painful hours of play, my son-in-law happily went bankrupt, ending his own misery. The world's longest game carried on with me holding tight to my only property, *Boardwalk*, after surrendering my one *Railroad* and the *Electric Company*. I breathed a sigh of exaltation when my youngest son, for whom I felt so sorry at first, robbed me of Boardwalk, allowing me to take a permanent break thanks to my financial disaster. He soon won the game going from rags to riches. Hallelujah.

There's a reason why people so rarely finish a game of Monopoly. It's very stressful. It took over a decade for us to play the game again. If we space it out like our last hiatus, it will be back in the box until 2026.

## Bedspread Mountain

Just when I got good at ignoring dishes in the sink, sitting on X-Box controllers without squealing, and breaking up fights between my son's youthful cat and our old feline, college break was over and quiet time returned with a bang. The nest emptied one birdie at a time as the trio headed out on different days this go-round, allowing my mind to prep for the impending roominess of our big old farmhouse and the front yard vacant without cars scattered around.

My youngest daughter, Sarah, and I spent a couple of her last days at home de-cluttering her room. One yank of a pillow caused an avalanche of giant fabric blobs of bedding collapsing on our heads from the closet shelf. When Bedspread Mountain was on the floor, one more tug brought down stuffed dogs and an enormous alligator pillow.

Lord have mercy! It was crammed up there like a football team in a Volkswagen Beetle. How many years of bedding and critters could a closet hold? At least a decade, since this twenty-one-year-old lass was once a ten-year-old girl all snuggled up into some of this softness. Even longer seeing some baby blankets in the pile.

A color-coordinated organization guru, Sarah had already spread orange sticky notes across her bed, ready to sort items by sheet sizes, blankets, and pillows. She had boxes standing by for the *attic worthy* and *donation* items.

We folded, stacked, and bagged up the best items and stretched out the oldest fitted sheets to see if their elastic made fun crunching sounds. If so, those oldies headed to the barn to someday transform into paint drop-cloths or plant-covers to protect the azalea blossoms from late North Carolina freezes.

The bedroom morphed into a magazine-worthy photo, with rearranged furniture, organized closets, and Sarah's paintings on the wall instead of in a stack. I think we were both surprised at how well we worked together and agreed on most decisions about what could go where. Years ago, the purging process wasn't so easy.

There was one slight problem. Far too many keepable items lined the hallway waiting for her daddy to make room for them in the attic. I'm pretty sure he didn't have as much fun as we did. Our attic is already filled much like Mary Poppins's bag exploding its contents when we attempt to find anything. What's a little more for the memory keeper cave? We'll purge again later and whittle it down some more.

That's one room down and two to go. I'm sure the boys would love to spend their future vacation days clearing out old belongings.

## Just Because I Used To Could

Now that the kids are gone and the house is still, I was inspired to go through my own closets, pulling out all kinds of *stuff* to sort, store, or donate. Since I don't need umpteen coats, I started my reverse nesting, I mean purging, in the bulging coat closet. Oh my, 1980s coats in two-sizes-too-small should send some fashion-conscious retro person over the moon with glee. I'd better get them out to the van before I decide to save them to show my future grandchildren.

## Parents Can Fly Too

The nest was empty for the summer. Nobody came home for work or an internship. That would be too ordinary. Somehow, we raised a bunch of adventure-seekers. Our now twenty-two-year-old triplets gallivanted all around the globe, often out of cell reach. *Did they do that on purpose?*

Our son Joe practically lived on football fields, in high school gyms, and on buses for three months. He trained and traveled with the Boston Crusaders of Drum Corps International, performing and competing against other competitive marching bands in over thirty stadiums across the United States. They practiced daily in extreme heat and showered in locker rooms before competing in the evenings. They occasionally slept in a bed or on gym floors but usually slept on the bus enroute to the next city or state. Joe preferred the extra legroom of sleeping on the floor beneath his seatmate who curled up on the bus seat. That sounds a wee bit uncomfortable.

Our daughter Sarah studied yoga in Bali, became a real life yoga teacher and checked out neighboring Australia before heading back to teach in the North Carolina Mountains. Our son Sam hiked the Himalayas and explored Hong Kong and China on his way to Australia. There he lived as a biology exchange student. Thank heavens our oldest daughter, Danielle, and son-in-law, Ben, the original models of world travelers, settled close by so we could heap all our love and affection on them. Lucky couple.

Even though our nest wasn't full for the summer, somehow, when school started in the fall, it was like a renewal of the Empty Nester Club card. Those same empty bedrooms and quiet house feelings rose up as the trees prepared to let go as well. It's gotten better though, as we've wised up with age. This fall we came up with a solution to singing the Empty Nester Blues at home.

We decided to leave it. Home, I mean. I'm serious. We traveled to watch Joe's incredible band compete in Winston Salem, North Carolina, and to see the finals in Indianapolis, Indiana, in August. They placed fifth out of forty bands, not an easy feat.

We spent time in the North Carolina mountains with our daughter Sarah once she returned from the other side of the world. She even taught me a few yoga classes. I was by far her worst student.

I'd teased our son Sam, saying, "When you choose your study abroad location, plan on us coming to visit. Make it a fabulous, travel-worthy place." He probably thought I was joking. Ha!

He did just that. He chose Sydney, Australia, as far across the earth as he could go. He chose the place that would cost the most in time and money to get to him. *I don't think he did that on purpose. Or did he?*

Anyway, quick as our cat smacks our grand dog's nose, we decided to book flights and hotels so we couldn't change our minds. No place is too far when we need to fly out of the nest to see what's happening with our birds. And then there's our oldest daughter and her husband fifteen minutes away, close enough that we can all flutter in and out of each other's nest at a moment's notice.

I think we're getting the hang of this empty nest thing. While the young birds explore the world, we empty nesters can be adventure seekers, too. And if our travels happen to take us in the vicinity of the kids now and then, it's all the better.

# Mom's Wisdom

## A Surprising Memory Aid

At 90 years young, my mother should be teaching her memory techniques to senior homes nationwide. She uses a kitchen table candy dish filled with dark chocolate Hershey Nuggets for more than maintaining healthy cholesterol levels. If she wants to remind herself to take the trash can out to the street, she sets one nugget on the table. Since it's out of place in her ultra-organized house, she'll see it and remember.

There's no way a wandering piece of memory candy would work in our house. When our family visits Mom, we've ruined her system more than once by putting the candy back in the dish. Well, OK, let's be honest. Sometimes we eat it. One might say we younger folks forget to remember her memory aid.

Once, when Mom was trying to remember that the exterminator was coming, she heard a candy wrapper crackle and she said, "You just ate the bug man." Then, from her special recliner, she flipped a coaster across her elevated feet to leave on the floor as her backup memory plan.

I used to cram all my rings onto my left-hand wedding ring finger. The three ring circles were so annoying that I remembered unwritten items on my to-do list. I can't use that method anymore thanks to my menopausal, salt-sensitive swollen fingers.

When I'm too lazy to write a sticky-note, I use Mom's method and put an item in a weird place as a memory nudge. For example, I might wonder, *Why's that nasty sneaker on my dresser? Oh, yeah. So I'll take a walk.* It has to be odd to stand out amidst the other out-of-place objects in our house.

I even send myself an e-mail reminder now and then. The problem is, my email in-box has 547 unopened emails, so the hints the rest of the world already sent smother my to-do's. Maybe I should use that reminder app on my phone, if only I could remember how to do that.

On a recent visit with Mom, when I spotted a drink coaster on the white carpet between her unoccupied trendy leather recliner and the kitchen, I bent over to pick it up. A voice from the adjoining sunroom said, "Don't you move my coaster. Remember, tomorrow's trash day."

Looking up from her homemade drop-biscuit-strawberry shortcake snack, she grinned.

Of course it is. Silly me. I reach for a nugget. Might as well lower my cholesterol since she's switched to coasters.

## Fish and Company

My mom, better known as Mama Lois or Lolo, was a little too perky when she called, after driving three hours from our house in Charlotte back to her home in Whiteville, near the North Carolina coast. We held her hostage at our house for longer than her usual short visit. She always says that fish and houseguests start to smell after three days. That saying bears lots of truth, but Mom is not the average guest.

Except for her medicinally thinned blood making her a human Popsicle, she's the most easygoing visitor ever. An expert tongue-biter, while the rest of us bicker over something ridiculous, she lifts her eyebrows, smiles, and pretends to read *TV Guide*. I'm pretty sure she's thinking that her oft-recited prediction came true. "Just wait till you have your own kids. You'll understand."

"I made it," she said on the phone once she arrived

home in Whiteville. "I got really sleepy, so I stopped about halfway at Hardee's and caffeined up. I hit the drive thru and had a coffee and cookie picnic in the parking lot."

"You didn't even get out to stretch your legs?" I asked.

"No. But I changed my new shades for my old ones and that did the trick. Those new black lenses wear out my eyes."

"You know they have bathrooms in Hardee's," I said, amazed at her bladder skills.

"Why would I go in their germy potty when I have a clean one at my house?"

It took all the mind-games and guilt-infliction skills she passed on to me to keep her a few extra days beyond Thanksgiving. She normally helped prepare and eat the Thanksgiving meal, then eat leftovers and a turkey sandwich supper before heading for home the next day.

Our oldest daughter, Dani, rushing home from her first holiday with her future husband's family in Ohio, was adamant that Mama Lois should stay to visit with her. I told her I'd do my best.

After breakfast, Mom said, "By the way, I'm getting ready to go. You've got enough going on without me getting under foot."

"Mom, that's crazy. Dani is rushing back to eat lunch with you and if you're gone, she'll be so disappointed. You're worried about my heart rhythm being out of control now; there's no telling how spasmodic it'll be if you leave and I have to deal with your sad granddaughter."

"Oh, stop," she said. "Of course, I'll stay and see Dani since she's on her way. And we sure don't want your rhythm out of whack."

She raised one eyebrow at me just like she did from her church pew years ago when I was giggling in the choir loft instead of listening to the preacher. I argued at the time, "We were behind the preacher and people should have been looking at him, not me."

Mom loves to visit, but she also loves her home. She cranks her heat up to 75 and sleeps well in her own bed. There are no peri-menopausal daughters with hot flashes or teens banging cabinet doors making school lunches at 6 a.m., debating who got the most turkey before the package was empty.

Mom was thoroughly entertained visiting in our *hangout house,* watching umpteen high schoolers move from X-box to movie to eating frenzy, hearing their uninhibited conversations and seeing their mountains of holiday homework.

Much less shocked at questionable language than while parenting my brother and me, I heard Mom use the word "butt" and then she laughed, saying, "I've never said that word in my life." Oh, my gosh, we're wearing off on her. If she ever says "OMG" or "That really sucks," I may never let the kids be around her again. We're such bad influences.

## Just Because I Used To Could

With Mom back home in her beloved routine, the kids ramped up the volume of their deliberations on everything and their blood and guts TV dramas to normal decibels. Rough around the edges as we are, when Mom comes, we all show a little more class. Maybe she stayed longer because fish and hosts don't smell so bad anymore.

## I Just Realized I'm Old

"Lisa, I just realized I'm old. How did that happen?" Mom asks.

"Beats me," I say. "You may be up there chronologically, but you sure don't act it. You and Betty White are 'Da Bomb Diggity.'"

Mom's ninetieth birthday sneaks up on us all. Unbelievable for all who know her and she can't believe it either. If nobody lets on about her age, people continue thinking she is much younger than her nonagenarian status, confirmed only by her birth certificate.

As it is, we use her age to shock folks just to see their expression. Like an acquaintance named Bessie who is digging through the fried chicken in the buffet and telling Mom about *So and So who is really elderly, and still driving.*

"Well, I'm almost ninety-one," Mom tosses out with a smile.

The conversation stops while Bessie stares at her in disbelief. "You're not serious. Miss Lois, I never would have guessed it. You look so young."

"Well, I am. I can't believe it either," Mom says.

Oftentimes a person learns Mom's age and says

something like, "Are you still driving?" or "Do you still live in your house?"

Mom just grins, cocks her head sideways, and says, "Of course I drive and still live in my house."

She tells me that people sometimes switch to baby talk when addressing her. At that, she puts on her feisty-lady voice and changes the subject to what she considers a much more interesting topic. The person she's talking with.

"So, tell me what's happening with you," Mom says, always interested in others and preferring not to talk about herself. Maybe that's what keeps her so young, caring about people and things outside herself.

I've got a few years to become more interested in others than in my own self, but I sure hope to be like her when I grow up. She's one funny character and one heck of a role model. And even if the calendar adds up the years, Mom will never be old.

## Techno Granny

My cell phone rang. Mom calling. Scary since she rarely calls.

"Hey, Mom. Is everything OK?"

Mom said, "Nothing's wrong. I knew you'd worry if I called. But I do have a problem. I broke the brand-new TV. This TV might be big, but the remote buttons are tiny and there are too many of them. I pushed the wrong button and then all of a sudden, there was a message on the screen."

"What's the message say?" I asked.

"Well, it could have been threatening a plague of frogs for all I understand. It said press button this, that, or the other. I thought and thought about what to do, and I tried to look it up in the manual. Finally, I just turned the TV off. I'll just wait to turn it back on when you come this weekend. You can fix it for me."

I smiled, knowing she's under the mistaken impression that I'm a techy smarty-pants. I pretend I'm tech-savvy at home and show the kids some new thing I've mastered but usually they say, "Yeah, that's an old app nobody uses anymore."

In reality, if it requires more than a few brain cells

for me to figure out my computer, TV, or phone, I call on my own young adult kids to bail me out. If I fear I'll erase my entire computer by pressing the wrong button when it starts asking me tough questions, I often use Mom's method. I wait until my son-in-law is in town to fix it.

I faced an ethical dilemma. Should I have been honest and told her I'd just unplug it, wait, then turn the TV back on and hope the threat goes away? Should I have ruined the vision she has of me being tech savvy? She's the only one who thinks of me that way and I kinda like it. My super-duper e-mail and Instagram skills make me seem like I know what I'm doing. I'm not going to tell her that most kindergartners today are more tech-savvy than I am.

She has a TV in the kitchen and in her bedroom that she can watch until I get there in a few days. She's a fabulous artist so she could use more free time for drawing. Also, she likes to kick back in her reclining chair to read and check Facebook with her iPad, which she calls her Doololly. She's getting pretty good at Instagram and is a master at iPad Solitaire. She should be fine without her new TV.

I paused a minute, imagining Mom's surprise when I pretend to fiddle around behind the TV, unplug the cord, wait five minutes to turn her TV back on, and the message is gone from her screen. Then I imagined reality. Her raising that right eyebrow she always guilted me with as a kid. She'll probably ask me, "Would you like to explain why you didn't tell me to unplug it, wait, and turn it back on?" I'd better call her back now before she figures out how to reset it herself.

## Cursing Through the Alphabet

In my house growing up, the B word was *butt*, the S word was *stupid*, and the D word was *dang* or *dagnabbit*. I might get by with *doggonit* or *darn* if I was really upset or talking about repairing a holey sock. The F word was *fart* and the C word would've been *crap*, two words I rarely use to this day. I could go through the entire alphabet and find words that I should not say in front of my parents or my grandparents. Or anybody else that they knew, which was most everybody in our small town of Whiteville, North Carolina.

My grandmother had a particular dislike for the word *nasty*. I really like that word. It covers a multitude of situations. The T word was *tail* as in "Do you need me to whip your tail?" My brother made up a song using my name and the H word, *hiney*. I don't know how he got away with that, but he did.

I remember being at an adolescent party and hearing other kids cursing. I decided to try it out too. I was standing beside one of the nicest girls I knew who probably had no cursing rules just like mine. What in tarnation made me decide to pull out the biggest, baddest words I knew and say them to her, I'll never understand.

Who knows the context but I said *GD* in probably the most ridiculous part of the sentence. Not only did I say the D word, but I tossed God's name into the phrase making it the worst thing I could've said. I think my friend looked at me like *what the heck are you doing*, but there's a possibility she looked at me because she couldn't hear me over the loud music. Either way, she kindly ignored it.

    I appreciate that, Catherine. To this day, I never said it again. That word combination, I mean. I can't be hypocritical and say that I don't occasionally throw out a word that would make my mother and grandmother cringe, but I hold back on the worst ones. Somehow, I know they would know.

# The Hands of Time

## Laying Out

  Dang, it used to be fun in the sun. People today would call it *tanning*; we called it *laying out*. Life was simpler when we could *lay out* all day and our only worry was getting a bad sunburn. Yes, sunburn hurt, but it was usually worth it unless it bubbled up and peeled, leaving our skin a splotchy mess. There was no mention of skin cancer back then, so ignorance was bliss. Our skin got as red as ketchup before we knew it. I have to admit, my mother knew best, warning me of sun damage before the world warned us about it. But did I listen?
  Growing up near the beach, my friends and I spread our towels between the sand dunes in late winter

and early spring. The dunes protected us from the stinging sand blowing into our eyes and sticking to our greasy skin. We could *lay out* long before it got warm enough out on the actual beach. A sunny day in February brought out the teens, nestled like litters of puppies among the dunes in North and South Carolina. This was way back in the old days when it was still legal to walk on sand dunes. Nobody knew about turtles nesting in the soft sand or worried about erosion of our wide beaches. I never saw a turtle until my middle-aged skin was way past tanning. Only an abundance of annoying little crabs we called sand-fiddlers.

With no wind to bother us, and the sun bearing down, we were bathing beauties or at least tanning teens and tweens soaking up the rays. We had a transistor radio. It stayed tuned to the *beach station* that tended to our skin safety with a DJ telling us every twenty minutes, "Time to turn before you burn." It didn't matter if the station played seventies rock or beach music, the DJs were the resident skin care specialists.

In spring, getting sunburned was our goal for going back to school the next Monday. Kids, please do as we say, not as we did. We didn't even care if our skin ended up peeling like an onion. It was worth the, "Ouch, I'm sunburned," laments when friends poked one another's skin to watch the poked spot switch from white back to red. It was worth all the pain when the sheets touched our fiery red skin that first night.

We tried to ease the burn by putting concoctions

on our skin. I recall sitting in my swimsuit in a bathtub while my friend poured liquids like milk or vinegar on my shoulders and back to deaden the sting. When that didn't work, we tried aloe plant slime. Maybe those methods helped a little but the best remedy by far was Solarcaine, which actually numbed the skin at least for a little while.

 Why didn't we just use sunscreen? The answer is, there wasn't such a thing. We had *Coppertone* and *Sea and Ski* suntan lotions and other such brands that might moisturize our skin, but did nothing to protect from a burn. *Hawaiian Tropic Dark Tanning Oil* was life changing, helping us either tan faster or burn faster depending upon the skin type. We all smelled like coconut oil and the sand stuck to us like flour to chicken ready for the fryer.

 There were some die-hard tanners who mixed baby oil and iodine together to enhance their tan, but I think the iodine just dyed the skin a nice reddish-brown. I knew a few people who used actual motor oil for tanning lotion and they were as dark as a white person could get. Perhaps I shouldn't share that and give any young people ideas they don't already have. Like that could happen.

 My proudest attempt at tanning was with one of my best friends, whom I'll name so she can share credit for our ingenious idea. My friend, Mimi Turbeville and I decided since cocoa butter was a new thing for tanning, and butter could brown toast, then butter should brown

## Just Because I Used To Could

us. Yep. We got out the Mazola and slathered ourselves in buttery spread. Laying out on beach towels atop the trailered ski boat in our back yard, we proceeded to roast ourselves. I can still smell the buttery aroma rising off our long white legs cooking in the sun. Let's just say coconut oil smells lots better.

## I Cry at Everything

 Where are my sunglasses? I'm so tired of hearing from my family how I tear up at everything. Nobody takes me seriously anymore. I used to be the wise one—the Gandhi at the top of the mountain. People used to climb into the thin air of my home office to hear sage advice about clothes, friends, dates, music, homework, banking, and the cosmos, the meaning of life. I knew how to ask all the right questions to guide the seeker in finding his or her own truth. That Master's degree in Counseling was worth a little bit at least. That degree in Education gave me a tiny fragment of credibility with my own kids and the extras I accumulated along the way.

 But something happened. Peri-menopause. It has turned me into a bundle of tears. I used to cry at appropriate times, like funerals and coffee commercials. Now, if my kids get snarkier than usual, voices raising an octave or two, they trouble the waters of my last nerve and my eyes fight those infernal tears. I try to convince the family that I'm not super sensitive, and that my tear ducts are actually connected to my anger button, and if they harass me about crying, my eyes might fill with fire instead of tears.

Where are those sunglasses? I need to go outside where nobody can see my floating eyes. I want to be with my dogs. They understand. I can sit in the swing, take a walk, or lie on the sidewalk in the sun. It might look like I've had a heart attack and scare somebody but it's lovely to have these dogs come check me for vital signs. At least somebody cares. They still think I am wise and wonderful. They sit and look at me with eyes that say "You, Mom, are the woofiest of all." And that makes me smile and, of course…tear up.

I wonder if Gandhi cried. I bet he cried about deep problems like war and hunger. I cry at everything. Hallmark movies, dogs eating peanut butter, public snarkiness. It's not fair. I finally told my kids to stop harassing me about hormones and menopause. I said, "Your brains are not even fully developed. When you turn twenty-five and that peanut brain is fully grown, then we'll chat. I should be over my menopause by then. So there!"

## Whose Hands Are on My Keyboard?

I wanted the bones on top of my third-grade hands to show through like Miriam's. She sat next to me in homeroom, and I admired her long fingers and thin hands. The bones shown in the top of her hands just below the silver Timex watch on her left wrist and the silver charm bracelet on her right. My hands had dimples instead of knuckles and my charm bracelet didn't look the least bit dainty on my pudgy wrist.

It took several decades, but I got my wish. Now, when I see my hands on the keyboard, sometimes I wonder whose they are. The bony, speckled hands typing away sport my mother's silver ring, reset with her diamond in the middle and her mother's two diamonds on either side. More bling than I normally wear, it makes me smile to look at that ring and think of my two favorite women.

Only pudgy if I've eaten too much salt, my hands now bear the signs of the dreaded sun damage Mom warned me about. I should have listened to her. The crepe-textured, thinning skin with sunspots some people call liver spots says, "I told you so," even if Mom doesn't say a word. I'm pretty sure she's smiling inside when I complain about my spots.

My grandmother preached sun protection even more and kept her hands, arms, and face protected, wearing gloves, long sleeves, and a wide-brimmed hat when she was in the sun for long. Vanity or just wisdom kept her skin beautiful for eighty-some years. That and a liberal dose of Vaseline slathered all over her porcelain face at bedtime. She was ahead of her time using natural remedies. Many times, I watched her cut a lemon in half and rub it all over the backs of her hands to fade age spots. Then she'd dig her nails into the lemon to bleach the tips white, which is now a popular thing to do.

My fingernails look a little like my dad's, with vertical age ridges and white tips. He used his nails like a knife to puncture, and then slice through the tough, brown packing tape that sealed huge cardboard boxes of shoes, boots, and purses delivered to his retail store. His nails must have been calcium-rich and strong as, excuse the pun, nails, just like he was, tearing into those cases of merchandise for forty years.

Today, I look at my aging hands and try not to think of thinning skin and age spots, but instead I think of my parents and grandparents and the hard work that went into raising and supporting our family. Age has allowed me the wisdom to know that it was hard work. I take comfort knowing my own hands deserve all the character lines and spots they have today.

## Lisa Batten Kunkleman

 I wonder what my childhood friend Miriam's life has been like. I wonder what her hands look like now?

## Crow's Feet, Chicken Arms, and Turkey Necks

Is DAS, Degenerative Aging Syndrome, meant to discourage procreation, eliminate conceit, and encourage humbleness? It's not so easy to be cock-of-the-walk when we glance in a store window expecting to see our thirty-year-old self and instead spy our old Aunt Gertrude or Uncle Abe sporting our clothes. Seriously, who is that old person?

When the aging process starts, we often notice crow's feet, chicken arms, or turkey necks. What's the deal with all the flock and poultry names? Aren't we supposed to be more like monkeys than birds? On second thought, some of us start growing hair on our faces, backs, and ears, a bit ape-like.

Does Mother Nature get a kick out of taking our crepe-like canvas of skin and painting on age spots and pasting on skin tags? And what about our shrinking eyes and crinkled lips? Everybody enjoys lipstick bleeding up the thinning lip lines and heading for the nose.

It must be quite a challenge for extra-beautiful people when they become more average looking. When beauty and metabolism head for the Hollywood hills and carb cravings creep in, maintaining the façade and keeping it all lifted could be a full-time job. All that nipping and tucking and lipo-sucking sounds awful. It can make a person glad to be average.

I've noticed some people start out a bit plain looking or downright unattractive and morph somehow so they look pretty darn good as they age. That seems fair.

If we're fortunate enough to reach middle age, we'll likely experience difficulty with some things we used to take for granted. Like sprinting up stairs, squatting and getting back up, or reading microprint on medicine bottles. We'll also note some improvements we never expected. Like freedom from daily leg shaving and less oily hair. That is, if one has hair. Many of us can wear clothes more than once without smelling like a sweaty adolescent basketball player.

If you're like me, do you no longer care much about what other people think? Do you realize we can act goofy and even a little eccentric? Do you realize we can become a funny old character that people gravitate toward instead of shying away from? Cut loose and cut up. It's OK. Blame it on age.

My ninety-year-old mother shares her aging tips with me. One of her best is using gray eye shadow to coat her scalp where the hair is thin. She also encourages rotating and flexing feet while relaxing in a recliner. It makes getting up and walking much easier. I've tried both and she is right, as always.

## Just Because I Used To Could

Oh, Mother Nature, what a shaky brush you use, but I'm pretty happy to be alive to sport those wrinkles, extra pounds, skin tags, age spots, and even a few crowns. The fake teeth type, not a tiara. I'm not especially thrilled about plucking facial hair to keep from looking like Tom Selleck in his giant moustache or Abe Lincoln with his beard. My very blond Scandinavian friend, Kathy, was shocked to learn that I could be "The Bearded Lady" if I misplace my tweezers. I'm sure she has some displaced hair but can't see it since it's light. Oh to be blond.

Now about those poultry metaphors. I'm delighted that my chicken legs need much less shaving even if my turkey neck and goozle require plucking. We have to take our perks where we can get them. As much as we fight getting older, people will stop aging when chickens stop making eggs and start needing lipstick.

## There's a Babe Under There

    Is it wrong to envy young people's satin skin, flat abs and lack of sag? I realize I had my youth already. I was reasonably cute and thin but at the time I thought I was plain and plump. As I look back at photos and the sizes of my life, I wish I could have told my young self, "Girl, you need to stop complaining. And stop that stupid chocolate milk and Captain's Wafer diet. You should see how much padding you'll hang onto after having four kids. Now that's something to whine about."

    I had an aha moment recently as I stepped out of the shower, reflecting on my midlife body in matching purple bra and let's be honest here, granny panties. I usually get on with covering up all that *me* in the mirror image, but this time, I noticed something interesting.

    I noticed how good my skin is on my upper arms. Yes. I just gave myself a compliment. These are the same jiggly arms I never show because a girl called me "Jell-O Arms" in elementary school. I didn't call her "Pencil Girl" but I could have.

    That white arm skin is fairly untouched by the sun's ultraviolet rays thanks to my mother's ominous sun warnings and swimsuit cover-ups for the past twenty years. Looking down I saw my upper legs are unblemished too.

It's almost a shame to only show the world my sun-damaged self. People don't know how youthful I am under all that cloth. It's like my own personal secret, that hidden smooth skin with the youthful glow. More like a blinding, white snow bank.

Oh, and when I turned to look over my shoulder, I realized that under those granny panties, there was skin that had never, ever seen the sun. I remembered the phrase, *soft as a baby's bottom.*

So it seems parts of me are in fine youthful condition. Keeping things under wraps is finally paying off. Another perk of aging discovered. Hallelujah.

## Just Because I Used to Could, Doesn't Mean I Should

If a horse named Mojo reared up like a wild bronco with a twenty-year-old man in the saddle, would you expect a fifty-something woman to get into that same saddle? Just because I was limber enough to get my foot up to the stirrup on this gargantuan horse didn't mean I should. His pouty pink bottom lip and shaggy winter coat gave him a cuddly, gentle look.

Seeking a companion for our lonely mare, whose field mate recently died, my kids and I were test-riding Mojo at my friend Pam's pasture. After switching out his bit, I got on his black and white speckled back assuming the bucking was history. He didn't flinch when I mounted, and he walked with my slightest heeltap. Perfect. What a sweetie. We rode around the pasture and bypassed two pokey riders. Approaching a mucky place, I guided Mojo off the trail and through the trees to stay on drier ground. Bad plan. I realize now the new bit made no difference, and Mojo probably needed a horsey dentist. Too late.

As I turned him left, he headed for the open gate toward the barn and pulling back on the reins made it worse. He wasn't slowed one bit (no pun intended) by my five-syllable Southern "Whoa" either. I was determined he wouldn't take me into the barn and whack my head on the doorframe but my attempts to stop or turn him meant he bucked higher.

I thought about jumping off, but feared being stomped to death so I flopped around like a city slicker on a mechanical bull. Since the bucking ride didn't stop, I gave in to gravity, which pulled me off to the left. I aimed for ground, as far away from Mojo as possible so I wouldn't end up looking like road kill. The hard, damp ground met my left knee and hip, and I caught myself with my left arm. Man, was that a jar. A shock shot from my back up into the base of my head, followed by a tingle like I've never experienced.

While I assessed my mobility, Mojo settled and stood there, sweet and innocent, like a big dog with a saddle, looking down at me. My young adult kids were frantic, yelling for my medical stats, so I stood up and walked toward them. Channeling my best John Wayne swagger and attitude, I said, "I lost my Mojo." Then, "He didn't like that bit even a little bit."

Relieved, they all laughed, except one. While my son, Sam, described my fall as pretty graceful, my oldest daughter, Danielle, was completely unimpressed with my graceful fall. She said through tight teeth and with misty eyes, "I bet you never had to watch your mother get bucked off a horse! It was horrible. I thought you'd die."

"Nope, I never had to do that. I'm sorry I scared you. I scared me, too," I said. She hugged me tight for a good while.

As I was brushing myself off, Pam, who has been thrown countless times, led me to sit on a log to watch the kids ride the safer horses. She whispered, "You need to fill the tub with hot water and soak in Epsom Salt 'cause we don't bounce back like we used to. One good thing about being over fifty is, if you fall off a horse, you can just lay there."

"Well, thank the Lord for that. Aging does have its perks," I said.

Twenty-four hours later, after a medicated sleep that lasted till lunchtime, I sported an immobile shoulder, a tattered wrist, and a rainbow-colored knee that I now know will be an inconvenience for years to come. A torn meniscus to remember Mojo by.

I could have injured my shoulder reaching behind the dryer for a lost sock, or I could have been thrown off a horse at fifty-two. I know that just because I used to could, doesn't mean I should, but since I survived the incident, I sure am glad I did.

Is there a time to stop risking injury from activities we used to love? A time to say, "No, I'm good. Y'all have fun without me." Maybe. I won't get back on Mojo, that's for sure. I'm pretty sore but it was worth it all to see the photo my future son-in-law, Ben, snapped as Mojo flung me from my saddle. Who knows, someday I might use that picture for a book cover.

# Acknowledgements

During and after writing this book, I found that the list of people to whom I owe thanks is longer than the guest list for a Charleston wedding. Knowing people are busy, I've condensed my acknowledgements to a mere morsel of what they should be. That means if you ever talked to me about this book or my writing or laughed at something I've written, please know that I'm thanking you publicly now and forever in my heart. You know who you are. I can't name you because at my age, I'd forget someone, and we'd be back in middle school feeling slighted. I love you all.

I'd like to thank those who have suggested, firmly, for many years that I should write a book. Peer pressure can be a wonderful thing, Marcie.

I thank my writing teacher and mentor, Maureen Ryan Griffin, for the smiles, suggestions, and praises for nearly two decades. To my Under Construction classmates from the past and in the present, thank you for all the critiques we've shared. It's a fun process, working together and learning from each other's ideas and writing skills. I especially appreciate the editing skills and honest opinions of Rachelle McClintock, Kathy

Brown, and my critique group members on the pieces selected for this book.

Special thanks go to my classmates who have already mastered this book publishing experience and have advised me along the way: Kathy Thorson Gruhn, Kim Love Stump, Lisa Otter Rose, Bridgett Bell Langson, and Cheryl Boyer.

My greatest thanks goes to my family, all of whom have supported my book writing dreams for decades: To my mother Lois, who has been waiting a lifetime to hold this book. To my husband, Dan, for his tireless reading, listening, and sharp-eyed-editing. I am not surprised since he notices the smallest details missed in editing every TV show. We watch a replay in slow motion and sure enough, the same car passes in every scene and a plate is full, then empty, then full.

To my oldest daughter, Danielle, and her husband, Ben, for help with the book cover, editing, and technical support, and to Sam, Sarah, Joe, and Emma, who I snagged for help anytime they stood too close and didn't seem busy.

To my brother, Mike, I give you my grateful thanks for traveling this life journey with me since birth. I'm thrilled to be not just your sibling but your friend. Thanks to all of you for trying to stay alert and help me out, again and again.

Finally, I am forever grateful for inspiration from the first female humor writer I remember, Erma Bombeck. She didn't know me, but I surely feel like I

## Just Because I Used To Could

know her. That's the beauty of the written word—those words can live on long after we are gone and reach many we will never get to know. I hope my words, like Erma's, give a few smiles and perhaps a laugh or two.

## About the Author

Lisa Batten Kunkleman, from Whiteville, a small North Carolina town, now lives outside the big city of Charlotte. A lifelong journal-keeper, history-lover, and amateur genealogist, Lisa feels compelled to write life stories. As a former guidance counselor and mother of four grown kids, three of which are triplets, and new grandmother of one irresistible little boy, Lisa is convinced that all of us have stories worth sharing. Her non-fiction work, a mix of serious and humorous tales, has been published in a variety of magazines and newspapers, and shared on NPR.

Lisa's children were thrilled to see she really was a writer when she won two non-fiction awards through the Charlotte Writers' Club and stood at the podium reading those pieces. She enjoys entertaining, enlightening, and engaging with readers through her blog, Lifestoriesandbeyond.com. With the triplets

## Just Because I Used To Could

finishing college and their oldest daughter and son-in-law starting their own family, Lisa and her husband, Dan, are getting reacquainted in their emptied nest. They're catching up on more than three decades of to-do items stored on the back burner and in their barns. They'll live on lake time, with or without a lake, as often as possible, and plan to travel when pet sitters are available for their farm full of dogs, cats, and horses. Lisa's looking forward to continuing to chronicle and share her own Life Stories and Beyond since every day is made up of new stories.

For more information about Life Stories and Beyond
Go to: https://lifestoriesandbeyond.com
Facebook: Lisa Batten Kunkleman
Instagram: @lisakunk

Email lisakunk@msn.com to request author appearances or for other personal correspondence.

May our stories scatter like seeds into the wind, landing hither and yon, taking root who knows where.
                                              Lisa Batten Kunkleman

www.ingramcontent.com/pod-product-compliance
Lightning Source LLC
Chambersburg PA
CBHW030325080526
44584CB00012B/719